We, the Puerto Rican People

We, the Puerto Rican People

A Story of Oppression and Resistance

by Juan Angel Silén

Translated by Cedric Belfrage

New York and London

Library of Congress Catalog Card Number: 70–158926

*Poems by Jorge María Ruscalleda Bercedóniz, José Manuel
Torres Santiago, Vicente Rodríguez Nietzsche, and
Iván Silén translated by Robert Márquez*

Manufactured in the United States of America

10   9   8   7

To Nancy, wife, friend, and compañera, because she was the inspiration that led me to write this book

Contents

Foreword   9
Introduction   11

I

Geography, History, Man   15
The Indian, the African, the *Jíbaro*   20
The Nineteenth Century   27
The Literature of Docility   36

II

A New Personality in History   49
North American Citizenship   55
Nationalism: Its Faults and Virtues   60
More on the Labor Movement   66
"Free State-ism"—The Popular-Democratic Party   70
The Loyal Opposition: "In Peace and Friendship"   75
The Korean War: The Counter-Revolutionary Army   81

III

The Roots of Power: The Economy   87
The Puerto Rican School   93
Religion: The Opium of the People   102
Women: The Double Oppression   105

IV

The Search for Achilles' Heel   113
The Enraged Generation   119

Foreword

In writing a book every writer has a purpose responding to an ideology, to a way of seeing the world. Wrapped in the writing of this essay is a whole experience that has been lived and learned from. The purpose took more solid form as the original manuscript was revised and a positive vision asserted itself—a positive vision of Puerto Rican history and of the task of struggling for independence that history has assigned to us as Puerto Ricans.

It would have been impossible to complete the book without the enthusiastic support of Wilfredo González, who encouraged and helped in the research plan I had undertaken. Nor would it have been written if I had not, by a happy decision, decided to teach: the theme would not have become such a preoccupation but for the many doubts expressed and gaps noted by my students at the Caserío San José and at the Dr. José N. Gándara School.

Challenged as I was to resolve these doubts, I wrote the first draft, which was read by Professor José A. Herrero, Dr. Luis Nieves Falcón, and Dr. Richard Levins. To them thanks for their stimulation and for the many criticisms that I thought valid and included in the final revision.

I am also grateful to the journal of political theory *La Escalera* for its many extremely useful articles; to César Andreu Iglesias for his essays on the labor movement; to Dr. Gordon Lewis for his brilliant *Puerto Rico: Freedom and Power in the Caribbean*; and again to Richard Levins for the positive influence of his many essays and articles on the Puerto Rican struggle.

I wish to mention too the work of Lidio Cruz Monclova —the *Historia de Puerto Rico (Siglo XIX)* (History of Puerto Rico in the Nineteenth Century)—and of Miguel

Meléndez Muñoz—*Estado Social del Campesino Puertorriqueño* (Social Condition of the Puerto Rican Campesino) —which simplified my labors. And finally, the person to whom the book is dedicated, my wife Nancy, who gave me her personal encouragement and understanding and was my severest critic.

To all these, and to those who guided my anxious steps in anonymity, my thanks.

Introduction

This is a book to explain the Puerto Rican people's fight for independence in a simple, clear, and reasoned way. Polemical in tone and open to debate, it is conceived in the form of an essay. Since its chief purpose is to educate, it is not a propaganda pamphlet. I have tried to give it the objectivity necessary for the detection of the errors of the struggle, not seeking to avoid confrontations with friends and enemies.

My approach is scientific, without an academic or university tone but with the clarity needed to understand problems and analyze processes. I do not interpret history on the level of individuals as does the traditional historian; for me history is defined by processes, and within each process there are classes in struggle and contradictions that need defining.

I do not pretend to interpret the Puerto Rican national character: in the colonial medium it is exceptionally hard to explain a river by a single spring. I do not aim to interpret history from the viewpoint of the "official truth" with which the system covers its "interpretations," but from the revolutionary viewpoint, which can see both the triumphs and defeats in a process.

The book's main character is the Puerto Rican: the people in their class expression of reality; the people, with their defects and virtues, in their search for a solution. Thus I analyze tendencies and contradictions between ideologies and within ideologies—to limit the analysis to one tendency or one contradiction would be to limit both content and methodology. If I did this I would be taking the interpretive road long taken by Puerto Rican literature

11

and history, as both colonialist and *independentista* writers have claimed to analyze our people's history.

Having neither a traditional, pessimistic, nor fatalist view of history, I write in the language of my generation. And I direct myself to all who have enough sensitivity, curiosity, and receptivity to hear and judge. I throw down a gauntlet to him who will examine, question, or accept. I am performing the duty of putting "a grain of sand" where others put lime. And so to the search for a positive view of the Puerto Rican . . .

New York, June 1971

I

These the ones responsible
for the daily chill and the perpetual hurry.
These the ones with a root
emerging between their teeth
and a hope embalmed on the high seas

. . . .

These the rogues of history
of time, of nausea,
the hysteria, the dollar, and conformity.

> Jorge María Ruscalleda Bercedóniz

Puerto Rico

Fajardo

Humacao

San Juan
Loíza
Río de Loíza
Río Grande de Loíza
Caguas
Guayama
Bayamón
Río de Bayamón
Cayey
Toa Baja
Dorado
Río de la Plata
Manatí
Aibonito
Salinas
Río Grande de Manatí
Coamo
Manatí
Ponce
Arecibo
Río Grande de Arecibo
Utuado
Guayanilla
Camuy
Yauco
Río
Yauco
Guánica
Lares
San Sebastián
Río Culebrinas
Río Grande de Añasco
Guanajibo
Aguadilla
Río
Mayagüez
Cabo Rojo

Geography, History, Man

To convey the pseudo-scientific notion of a "sad people," our literature has used our geography as a pessimistic *obbligato*. Schools and universities have used it to explain the political and economic situation that cripples us as a people—the first lesson a schoolboy learns is that we are small, as if our smallness were not something positive for grappling with the problems of communication, electrification, irrigation, and highways. In fact, aspects of our national reality which may have hindered progress in the last century, when scientific techniques at man's service were lacking, are positive today.

Let us look at our geography to see whether it has really been that of a sad people, or whether its exploitation by foreigners has not brought us the sadness of any colonized nation. Let us see whether our sadness is a product of natural disasters, as Salvador Arana Soto has said; of a climate which "melts our will," as Antonio S. Pedreira has said; or of the self-destructive impulse diagnosed by René Marqués. Is it true that we are special and different from the Latin American peoples? Surely whatever is special about us is the product of continuing colonialism and its rationalizations—its use of pseudo-scientific theories and decadent ideologies to affirm the superiority of the dominating people over the dominated. The Second Declaration of Havana made this point about another colonized Caribbean island: "What is Cuba's history but that of Latin America? What is the history of Latin America but the history of Asia, Africa and Oceania? And what is the history of all these peoples but the history of the cruelest exploitation of the world by imperialism? At the end of the last century and beginning of the present a handful of economically developed nations had divided the world among themselves, subjecting two-thirds of humanity to their economic and political domination. Humanity was thus forced to work for the dominating classes of the group of nations which had a developed capitalist economy."

One of the first descriptions of our geography is in *Memorias de Melgarejo* (1582). The island is described as "rough, mountainous, crossed by many rivers and streams which are extremely good and healthful"; there are also "seams of copper in many places and seams of tin, lead and other metals . . ." With regard to the shortage of gold, the author notes: "The land would otherwise be prosperous, well populated, and well supplied with the things of Spain, for with possession of gold nothing would be lacking." And about the climate: "It is very good and the same nearly all year round . . ." Thus a first impression of the island, its climate and waters was of a good and healthy land. The presence of commercially valuable metals was noted, as well as Spain's disinterest in an island without much gold—it was the hunger for gold that guided the discovery and conquest of America.

In Diego de Torres Varga's *Descripción de la Isla y Ciudad de Puerto Rico* (1647) we see how the author was immediately struck by what was good about our geography. Comparing Puerto Rico's "atmosphere and qualities" with the other Windward Islands, Torres Varga wrote that Puerto Rico "enjoys perpetual spring, with neither heat nor cold to disturb the constitution . . ." Of the land he wrote: "It is all very fertile and green . . . , fertile for whatever crop one wishes to plant in it . . ." He stressed the mineral resources—especially the copper—and noted the island's strategic military importance, which was to lead to its conversion into a fortress protecting the entrance to the Spanish routes to the Indies. In 1644 Fray

Damián López de Haro wrote of abundance, but also of the poverty in the *city*. He noted the isolation and penury of the natives who received nothing regularly from Spain; the abundance of fruits, shortage of money, high cost of commercial articles; the damage done to agriculture by storms and the attacks of the "enemy." He noted that the family survived "cheerfully, because what it lacks to sustain itself is compensated by the abundance of this country . . ."

In the chapter on climate and resources in his *Historia Geográfica, Civil y Natural de la Isla de San Juan Bautista de Puerto Rico* (1788), Fray Iñigo Abbad y Lasierra wrote of the "bountiful nature" that permits "all kinds of crops suited to warm countries" to be raised in the valleys— fruits, vegetables and roots which, "unaffected by the sun's heat, reproduce themselves all year round . . ." And Marshal O'Reylly—an Irish soldier who served the king of Spain and made a political, economic, and military study of the island—stressed in his *Memoria sobre la Isla de Puerto Rico* (1785) the fertility of the soil and the ingeniousness of some inhabitants for whom, living in modest abundance, problems of survival did not arise. Of the climate, he noted: "The heat is very moderate, the atmosphere very healthful" and favorable for both natives and Europeans. Of the land: "It is bathed by copious rivers which abound in good fish; in the mountains water is never lacking; there are fertile and bountiful plains, and two and even three harvests of corn, rice and other crops are raised every year . . ." He spoke of cotton, indigo, coffee, pepper, cacao, nutmeg, and vanilla; of timber for furniture in the mountains; of countless medicinal roots and herbs; and of a contraband business exceeding 43,000 pesos and of its importance in the island's development. He blamed the Spanish Crown for the "minuscule progress made by Puerto Rico," and noted the Puerto Rican's "inertia." He called Puerto Rico's sugarcane "the thickest, tallest, juiciest and sweetest in America . . ."

Where then is the geography of hunger that Rexford Tugwell, Puerto Rico's governor from 1941 to 1946, tells us about in his book *The Stricken Land?* In the seventeenth and eighteenth centuries Puerto Rico's chief characteristic was abundance, built on a diversified agriculture and an illicit trade—smuggling. What emerges from unprejudiced chroniclers and historians is that, in the period of its discovery, conquest, and colonization, the island was wealthy in climate, vegetation, crops, and soil. It was the absence of gold, once the small veins had been exhausted, together with Spain's centralized administration of its colonies and the fact that for over 200 years we were submitted to commercial isolation—the mercantilist policy of the Hapsburgs of Austria forced isolation on all the islands and especially on Puerto Rico—that led to the stagnation of our agriculture and industry and imposed a monocultural economy upon us. These policies were only accentuated when the United States dominated the management of sugar corporations, after our predominantly coffee economy collapsed at the end of the nineteenth century. And our forests were destroyed to make room for livestock and to increase the acreage for farming.

From the failure of Hapsburg mercantilism we passed to the absolutism of the Bourbon kings. Embroiled in wars and alliances against England, they transformed us into a military fortress. And when Spain's loss of its American mainland colonies improved our economic prospects in the nineteenth century, the situation in monarchical and feudal Spain, split by civil war, meant political instability at home and military governors overseas, men with unlimited powers but narrow visions, even for a colonial enterprise.

Where does the anguish about our geographical situation come from? Whence the lament about *taras?* * Some writers say that our racial mixture produced *taras* which deprived us of control over our destiny and over our wretched geography, and so we became "passive" and submissive.† Basically *ñangotado,*‡ resigned, fatalist, pacific, and tolerant—this is the Puerto Rican according to the deterministic, regionalistic, docility concept. He is supposed to have an inherited docility that has led him to accept the colonial regime.§ Some of the Puerto Rican historians, writers, and essayists who believe this have been relying on a determinism produced by theories which modern man, through science and technology, has discredited. Others have failed to explore the past for evidence of the people's victimization by a leadership which,

---

* *tara:* an indigenous word used by the intellectual elite to describe an inherited sickness or weakness.

† See Antonio S. Pedreira, *Insularismo: Ensayos de Interpretación Puertorriqueña* (San Juan: Biblioteca de Autores Puertorriqueños, 1934). Since the bourgeois leaders' praise of docility is no more than a wish that the worker and peasant be docile to *them,* the worker's docility is exaggerated and his rebelliousness minimized. Thus the standard literature takes the worker as a passive model—not as a worker but as a poor and humble man, not as producer but as a victim and a recipient of charity; and never as deserving respect. The bourgeois writer disparages what he purports to praise, justifying this by the Puerto Rican's alleged docility.

‡ *ñangotado:* a word used to describe the position in which the peasant traditionally sits and talks—hence, derogatively, used to describe a person who cannot stand up.

§ Antonio S. Pedreira and René Marqués belong to different literary trends and generations but fail equally to understand the phenomenon of Spanish colonialism and U. S. imperialism. Pedreira wants to blame geographical and biological, Marqués psychological, factors. Pedreira's *Insularismo* (1934) might be the biography of a sad and bitter man who still sees chinks of light. "El Puertorriqueño Dócil" is a summary of the deceptions with which a generation without faith in the future justifies its role.

because of its class origins, allied itself with foreigners to maintain its privileged "junior partner" position.*

As for us, we agree with the black leader Malcolm X, who said of his own people's history: "When you deal with the past, you're dealing with history, you're dealing actually with the origin of a thing. When you know the origin, you know the cause. If you don't know the origin, you don't know the cause. And if you don't know the cause, you don't know the reason, you're just cut off, you're left standing in mid-air. So the past deals with history or the origin of anything—the origin of a person, the origin of a nation, the origin of an incident. And when you know the origin, then you have a better understanding of the causes that produce whatever originated there and its reason for originating and its reason for being. It's impossible for you and me to have a balanced mind in this society without going into the past, because in this particular society as we function and fit into it right now, we're such an underdog, we're trampled upon, we're looked on as almost nothing." [1]

The Indian, the African, the Jíbaro

The raw material of our nation is the Indian, the slave, and the *jíbaro*.† These were victims of the forms of labor

---

* Thus when René Marqués uses contemporary literature as "proof" that Puerto Ricans are lost and damned, he does not understand that this reflects the crisis produced in the country by the capitalist transformation beginning in the 1950's.

† *jíbaro:* an indigenous word for the Puerto Rican *campesino;* in the Indian language the word means "being free."

imposed by the ruling class: the *encomienda,* slave, and *agrego* systems. Their voices can be heard in the indigenous rebellions; in the Negro conspiracies on agricultural estates; and in the struggle to abolish slavery that linked the slave to the Lares revolution of 1868, whose force came from the *campesino* masses. The *campesino* was the "subversive" at Lares. Terrorized in the repression of 1887, he formed the mobile corps of *macheteros** who fought in the Spanish-American War of 1898.

These were the men who built the seditious groups that rebelled against rural feudalism, and who, having no ideology, ended in "banditry" and fell victim to the new army, the army of the United States. These were the agricultural workers who burned the sugarcane and went out on strike under the Socialist Party's red banners, provoking the Unionist-Republican coalition against the "red peril." These were the men who filled the plazas to hear Pedro Albizu Campos; and these were the men who surged to the polls to back the social-justice slogans of the Popular-Democratic Party in 1940. So it is hardly accurate to speak of "a people remote from violence and politely peaceful," as does Antonio S. Pedreira, or of a people guided by a "self-destructive drive" compounded (according to René Marqués) of nationalism and annexationism.

Colonial violence is not the product of a people. It is used against a people by a ruling class that seeks to maintain an exploitative system beneficial to itself. As Sartre aptly tells us: "Violence in the colonies does not only have for its aim the keeping of these enslaved men at arm's length; it seeks to dehumanize them." [2] More specifically, colonial violence aims at liquidating the subject people's traditions, at replacing their language with another, at

---

* *macheteros:* wielders of *machetes,* the basic tool of the Latin American agricultural worker.

destroying the culture of the colonized while withholding that of the colonizer—and thus at brutalizing within a net of ambivalences and contradictions.

Many have distorted the simple life of our Indians into proof of their incompetence. It would be more appropriate to consider the relationship between man and nature in the life of our Indians; between their god-images (*cemis*) and the sacred mountain Luquillo; between their chief crop (the cassava or *yuca*) and their chief god Yuquiyú or Yucayú, and the name Yucayeque given to his village. The fact that these people were more attracted by colored beads than by gold is intimately linked to a man-nature relationship in which gold had no economic value.

In the context of a simple and almost routine life, the arrival of Europeans was something novel and out of the ordinary. The belief that Europeans were gods had to do with the cultural difference in time and space between Spaniard and Indian. Among the significant differences were clothing, metals, gunpowder, skin color, and the Spaniards' arrival from the sea in large ships. The Spaniards, hospitably received, imposed absolute dominion upon the native population. Christianization went hand in hand with *repartimientos** that overturned family life and simple habits, with foreign ownership of land, and with forced labor in the search for gold—all this in the name of Christian civilization. To appraise our Indians' behavior using "modern" thought-models is to let prejudice rule over judgment. Instead of condemning, a proper interpretation should seek the basic causes behind a historical process.

When the Indians began to protest, it was against a violence imposed by forced labor, against a religion which

---

* *repartimiento*: a system whereby the Indians were allotted to Spaniards as slave labor.

threatened their whole world, and against a European morality which threatened their legitimate customs. The first protest took the form of flight to the mountains; the Spaniard replied with violence, pursuit, and punishment.

A confrontation was not long in coming. In 1511, the Indians drowned a Spaniard named Diego Salcedo to prove that Spaniards were mortals, not gods. With his death armed rebellion broke out. It was bloody and treacherous, and major battles were fought against the Spaniards by Arawaks and Caribs. The battles of Río Coayuco (between the Aguada and Culebrinas rivers), of the Culebrinas valley, and in the province of Yagüeca (now Mayagüez and Añasco) live in our history. The immortal heroes of our first fight for liberty are the Arawak chiefs or *caciques* Agüeybana and Guarionex, who have passed into our literature and history deformed by Hispanists scornful of our true roots.[3] As one Puerto Rican historian wrote, "Force won the day, true; but the Puerto Rican Indian, defeated in combat, won the right to historical immortality: cowards do not fall as this people fell." [4]

Spain entered America with the seed of decadence in its bosom. American gold could not prevent its downfall; it was condemned to be a second-class power compared to England and France. By expelling Jews and Arabs after the war of reconquest against the Moors, Spain destroyed productive forces which it did not know how to handle. As Engels commented: "These . . . are isolated cases of conquest, in which barbarian conquerors have exterminated or driven out the population of a country and have laid waste or allowed to go to ruin productive forces which they did not know how to use. This was what the Christians in Moorish Spain did with the major part of the irrigation works on which the highly developed agriculture and horticulture of the Moors depended. Every conquest by a more barbarian people naturally disturbs the economic development and destroys numerous productive forces." [5]

While Spain's conquest of the new world was a step forward for the island in comparison with native civilization—the introduction of Spanish gunpowder and steel pulled the Puerto Rican Indian out of the primitive state in which he lived—reconquest of the Spanish peninsula had upset the productive forces and imperial Spain was destined to fail. In Puerto Rico the Indian began to disappear: war, epidemics (especially smallpox), and flight to other islands to avoid servitude dried up the primary labor source. And servitude—in the form of *encomiendas*° and *repartimientos*—presupposes possession of the means of labor by him who forces another to work.

The feudal-patriarchal philosophy of the Spaniards produced the *agrego* system. Without any land of his own the Puerto Rican *campesino* came under the jurisdiction of the "father of the *agrego*"—the feudal *señor*, fattening on the division of crops, who put his economic and political imprint on whatever was his property. The *campesino* was not paid for his work; he lived at the subsistence level and worked from dawn till dusk. The land belonged to the *señor*, who imposed his lordship just as the feudal *señor* of old had imposed his upon the medieval European serf. The *agrego* could not leave the estate on work days without the master's permission. He could not celebrate any of his traditional fiestas—dances, rosary processions, wakes, and so on—without permission. He had "freedom," but it was so surrounded by conditions and so neutralized as to be hardly worth anything. [6] He was subject to every economic crisis, which threw him out of work, ruined, and pauperized him.

° *encomienda:* a system whereby land was allotted to the Spaniards.

The African was brought to the island to work the mines, and became in our first historical stage the chief worker on Crown lands (*Hatos del Rey*) and big estates. Africans were essential for the development of the colony: they were the moving force of the sugarmills, the planters of ginger, the domestic servants. They were seen as pieces of property, and it was not till 1784 that the use of the *carimbo* brand, showing to whom they belonged, was abolished.

By 1553 there were 1,500 slaves; by 1834 there were 30,000. Contrary to the myth that abolition was won bloodlessly—an invention of the rulers to show the goodness of their hearts and the grandeur of their society at the time—slave conspiracies had erupted early in our history. The first revolt came in 1527. The authorities took due measures against the rebels and the *cimarrones*, slaves who had fled to the mountains and become a danger to the incipient colony's inhabitants. In 1796 fugitive slaves in the mountains were still a peril to the neighbors. The authorities meted out punishments ranging from the lash to the severing of hands and, in many cases, death.

In 1821, 1822, and 1825 rebellious plots were detected in Guayama and Ponce. In 1843 the authorities had to suppress a rising in the Toa Baja haciendas—which they did with the aid of slaves from neighboring haciendas.* Another plot was discovered in Ponce in 1848. Not until the Lares revolution, the first uprising for independence and demand for the abolition of slavery, on September 23, 1868, did the Madrid government, seeing how the black emancipation movement was linked with the Lares revo-

---

* The grandfather of José Celso Barbosa, José María Barbosa, won the Spanish government's Cross of Merit for his "valor" in helping suppress the Toa Baja slaves. See Antonio S. Pedreira, *Un Hombre del Pueblo* (San Juan: Imprenta Venezuela, 1937).

lutionaries, take the steps which led to the abolition of slavery in 1873.

In the twentieth century the *jíbaro* is called passive, tolerant, democratic, and docile—yet he is the same *jíbaro* who rebelled at Lares in 1868. As one well-known Puerto Rican expressed it: "The government suppressed the revolt and he [the *jíbaro*] suffered the consequent punishments, outrages, and coercions. He participated . . . in the events of 1887. He was beaten down. He was jailed and subjected to the most infamous and refined tortures to tell what he knew, to describe what he had not seen, to confess what no one had told him, to denounce his chiefs and leaders as conspirators, seditious rebels . . . And he was terrorized." [7]

It may be said that the *jíbaro* did not know what he was doing, that he was caught up in events. But the truth is that a natural imperative of sympathy, his whole background and history, identified him with certain movements. Because they were of Puerto Rican origin, these ideas aroused his confidence and led him to act generously and spontaneously. In the same way, the *jíbaro* who had rebelled and been terrorized became the mounted *guerrillero* of the Spanish-American War of 1898; the anonymous hero who fought "in the Villodos revolt, at Monte del Gato, around Guayama and Salinas, at Asomante, Guánica, Yauco, and Guayanilla, and withdrew to the center of the island with the mass of the Spanish army, always harassing the enemy." [8]

The comfortable ruling classes swore loyalty to Spain and, frightened of a war that might destroy them, retired to their country estates far from the theater of war. Their withdrawal proclaimed their neutrality. They ingratiated themselves with the North Americans as the Spanish troops and Puerto Rican *macheteros* retreated from the towns and cities. Puerto Rican historian Lidio Cruz Monclova describes the situation thus: "Some were moved by resentment of the painful, bitter, shameful tyrannies of the Spanish authorities. Others by roseate optimism from the many eulogies of the great United States which had been published throughout the century outside and inside the island. Others by ambition to become the new ruling class which the victors would need to buttress their power—for mutual antipathies engendered by the war had for the time being separated the old caste of big merchants from the government." [9]

The Nineteenth Century "*The golden age*"

The nineteenth century is one of the most interesting periods in our history. Many historians have called it our golden age. It was the century when the Puerto Rican national conscience flowered in two significant directions, that of reformism and that of separatism.

At the start of the century Puerto Rico was governed on absolutist principles. Economics and politics were completely centralized. The island was ruled like a fortress by a captain-general who had total control, both military and civil. His power extended into the economy and the judiciary; he was in charge of the royal treasury and its tribunal, and was a decisive influence in church affairs. His control was absolute also in matters concerning the island's security, where his power was in the form of *facultadas omnímodas*, powers granted by Spain to governments in the colonies. These were extended in 1810, revoked in 1811, and reaffirmed in 1825; they continued in effect until 1873. Spain was taking precautions to keep the Mexican and Venezuelan revolutions from influencing the Puerto Ricans.

From 1816 to 1825 the country's commerce was affected by the activity of South American pirates in the Caribbean. The United States and England began to show concern about this revolutionary activity, as the pirates attacked and plundered Spanish ships in Cuban and Puerto Rican waters, and by 1825 United States and English intervention secured Puerto Rico and Cuba as Caribbean military bases for Spain. This led in turn to an increase of the island's trade with the United States. As trade grew, local activity and production increased. Puerto Rico exported sugar, coffee (then the chief item of our economy), cattle and horses, timber, corn, oranges, hides, and rum. Imports included manufactured goods, machinery, wheat flour, rice, paper, petroleum, codfish, salt meat, olive oil, and soap. Commercial relations were maintained with Spain, the United States, the Lesser Antilles, France, Haiti, Holland, England, Italy, Mexico, Portugal, Santo Domingo, and other countries.

Despite the rise in trade and the activity it generated, the growing Creole class—located in the mountain coffee plantations—felt caught between the Spanish merchants, who had their commercial houses in San Juan and who benefited from the city trade boom, and the big feudal landowners, who were the main beneficiaries in the countryside. The income from customs duties was used for the garrison, the government bureaucracy, and administrative expenditures. Spanish governors were military men with absolute powers who dominated the political situation. Spain's policy was characterized by the abuses, despotic measures, and rigidity of the military.

One of the governors most distinguished by the abuse of his powers was Miguel de la Torre, who ruled the island from 1822 to 1837. His administration has been described as the dancing, gambling, and drinking administration. De la Torre was the Spanish commander defeated by Bolívar in the battle of Carabobo, Venezuela, in 1821. As governor he strictly regulated the citizens' lives and activities—for example, no one was allowed on the streets after 9 P.M.

Other absolutist governors who imposed a feudal policy in this period were Captains-General Miguel López de Baños, Juan Prim, and Juan de la Pezuela. López de Baños declared anyone without "property, profession or office" ᴀ laborer and ordered him to get a job and a master. Juan Prim, governor in 1847–1848, wrote the Negro Code—designed to head off abolition and nip any libertarian move in the bud—that imposed cruel punishments on blacks for minor offenses and crimes. Pezuela (1848–1851) set up a system of work-books, which had the effect of regulating labor and turning it into naked servitude. Anyone over fifteen without "profession or capital" was considered a laborer and had to register with a judge, who gave him his work-book. Employers wrote in the book the date on which the holder began and finished working, his wage, his conduct, and whatever else they thought worth noting. There was great resentment among Puerto Ricans at this system, which benefited the moneyed class at the expense of the dispossessed.

Puerto Rico's economy was so dependent on sugarcane, coffee, and tobacco that our agriculture was essentially limited to these three products. The farmable areas were divided into zones of monoculture, each featuring a product which brought high profits. The result was increasing deprivation and ever narrowing social conditions for our working masses. The governors' abuses, the slavery, the economic limitations, and the lack of civil liberties are among the reasons *some* Puerto Ricans raised their voices in protest. Separatism and reformism began to take shape in reaction to the Spanish straitjacket.

The first conspiracy to surface in terms of the separatist movement was in 1835, when a plot was discovered involving a captain and some sergeants and corporals who wanted to proclaim the Constitution of 1812. A plot by the brothers Andrés and Juan Vizcarrondo and Buenaventura Quiñones was discovered in 1838. The Vizcarrondos fled to Venezuela and the strangled body of Buenaventura turned up in El Morro fortress (he was thought to have been assassinated). Three sergeants and five corporals were shot in connection with this incident.

A barracks rebellion in the capital in 1867 resulted in the execution of a corporal, Benito Montero. The plot was linked to the abolitionist and separatist propaganda that was emanating from secret groups all over Puerto Rico. Revolutionary juntas were actively functioning in Lares, Mayagüez, San Sebastián, Camuy, and Ponce. (The first three of these were coffee-growing centers; Camuy was devoted to tobacco and Ponce to sugarcane.) In the aftermath of an uprising by artillerymen of the San Juan garrison, Governor-General Marchessi sent sixteen Puerto Rican liberals into exile, including Dr. Ramón Emeterio Betances and Licenciado Segundo Ruiz Belvis. These two, disobeying Marchessi's orders, slipped across the channel to Puerto Rico's outer island Mona. On July 9, 1867, they reached Santo Domingo, seeking arms for the revolution they had helped prepare in Puerto Rico. Ruiz Belvis was murdered in Chile, where he was seeking support. In September a price was put on the head of Betances, who was known to be back in the island conspiring in Morrillo in Cabo Rojo. Measures were taken to capture him but he escaped by way of Guánica.

From the then-Dutch island of St. Thomas he issued the first revolutionary call, "The Ten Commandments of Liberty," the first of which was the abolition of slavery. On December 22 his second proclamation was circulating in western Puerto Rico: "Puerto Ricans! An end to Spanish domination . . . !" On January 2, 1868, he drew up the "Provisional Constitution of the Puerto Rican Revolution" in Santo Domingo, where he learned of the United States' offer to buy Cuba and Puerto Rico from Spain. He sailed for the Dutch colony of Curaçao where he had 500 rifles cached. In August he wrote: "The separation is made: for us, our beautiful Borínquen [Puerto Rico]; for them, the gorges and crags of Sierra Morena!" And then in September 23, 1868, he received the news of the failure of the insurrection at Lares.

The *Grito de Lares* marked the birth of our Puerto Rican nationality. It was the voice of a Puerto Rico that had its own interests and its own consciousness. Those interests had collided with the interests of Spain, with the Spanish government, bureaucracy, army, and commercial monopoly. The revolutionary nucleus was recruited from among our *campesinos*. The *jíbaro*, as the man who produced the coffee on the hacienda, was cast in the leading revolutionary role of the anonymous hero fighting for the demands of his class. In joining the revolution he put his protest on the line against the privileges and luxury of a tiny minority. From that day on, the *jíbaro* was the people.

In 1870 political parties began to be organized. Conservatives and traditionalists united in a conservative party, which had the support of the chief Spanish families on the island. Elements of the Creole class formed the Liberal-Reformist Party. But in that year only some 4,000 persons out of a population of 650,000 participated in elections. This was an essential aspect of Puerto Rican political life at the time: elections and parties responded to interests closely connected with the owning classes, the

Creoles and Spaniards; the masses remained apart from activities which did not affect them in any way.

In 1874, under the governorship of General Laureano Sanz, the Civil Guard was created as a police instrument to use against Puerto Ricans. Censorship was imposed with abolition of the printing laws; rights of assembly and association were eradicated; teachers were hounded and the Civil Institute of Secondary Education was shut down. From 1875 to 1885 a procession of ten Spanish governors heaped new persecutions and limitations on top of the old tyrannies.

Beginning in 1883 a polemic developed between the two main tendencies within the Liberal-Reformist Party, the assimilationists and the autonomists. The assimilationists wanted to make Puerto Rico a Spanish province with the same rights and duties as the provinces in Spain. The autonomists wanted Puerto Rico to have its own government, one in which Puerto Ricans would run their own internal affairs. By 1887 the autonomists, under Ramón Baldorioty de Castro, were gaining ground and a convention in Ponce's La Perla theater approved a program calling for an autonomous government. General Romualdo Palacios arrived as governor on March 23 of that year. Under his administration the autonomists were accused of being revolutionaries and separatists. They were terrorized by threats, beatings, jailings, and physical tortures. Baldorioty de Castro, who advocated autonomy on the lines of Canada, was put in jail and kept there until the Spanish government recalled General Palacios.

Baldorioty de Castro represented the most radical sector of the Creole class. His vision of autonomy inevitably led him to see the need for independence if Puerto Rico was to be freed from the Spanish straitjacket. On the other hand, autonomism as envisioned by Muñoz Rivera, who represented the Creole class's most conservative element, would end up in assimilationism. The political ambivalence of Muñoz Rivera's autonomism showed the Creoles' incapacity to assume any role other than that of junior partner of the Spanish exploiters. The autonomists limited themselves to requesting participation in exploiting the country. From 1889 to 1897, autonomism, led by those most conservative in action, most aristocratic in essence, and only revolutionary in appearance, expressed the "pragmatic policy" of Muñoz Rivera.[10]

But the situation of the Puerto Rican people—victims of an asphyxiating administrative policy, of a bureaucracy, of, as Cruz Monclova has put it, "filing-cabinet routines, running out of control under the hierarchical, nepotistic, and political-favor setup"—was far removed from ruling-class ideology. Bureaucracy drained the island's budget; bribery and corruption characterized the municipalities. Mayors helped themselves with a big spoon to the extent that teachers' salaries often went unpaid. Unrepaired roads became impassable, further isolating the bulk of the population. A trip from San Juan to Ponce took twenty hours. There was a coach-transport system, but with pot-holed highways and rising rivers it barely functioned. At that, the transportation was for the privileged few who could afford it.

The railroad made its appearance in 1889 but its extension and use were slow. Health services improved relative to earlier times, but located as they were in towns, with roads bad and few, they had no positive effect on *campesinos,* who continued succumbing to diseases of all kinds. The 600-odd public schools did not suffice for the children who should have been being educated. Some private elementary schools and institutes for specialized technical and professional education were started in various parts of the island, but the masses continued to wallow in superstition and illiteracy. The administration of justice was a maze of complicated procedures, of interminable and costly lawsuits. Postal, telegraph, cable, and telephone service began only in 1897. Banks were opened and began to extend credit to the island's agricultural, industrial, and commercial interests: the Banco Popular in San Juan in 1893, the Banco de Crédito y Ahorro Ponceño in Ponce two years later.

The religious unity typical of colonial life was threatened with the arrival of Protestants, Spiritualists, and Masons. In fact, a gubernatorial circular to the mayors in 1897 linked Masons and Spiritualists with the revolutionary movement in Yauco.

The intellectuals began to worry about the growth of a 953,243 population; the "excess" would become a "problem" by 1898.

The comfortable classes received the education the colony offered, traveled, amused themselves, speculated with their capital through banks and gambling, and acquired new tastes. Civic associations, clubs, casinos, and circles of a recreational type mushroomed from 1886 on. Porcelain vases, Louis XV furniture, kerosene stoves, and Singer sewing machines became the marks of social distinction in bourgeois and petty bourgeois families. They set their tables with an abundance of meats, shellfish, and a variety of desserts, many, such as Spanish nougat, crystallized fruits, and French cookies and biscuits, imported. Fashions were set in Madrid, Paris, or London and were in silk, brocade, crepe, and tulle. Cosmetics ran the gamut from powders to soaps "to beautify and retain smooth, velvety skin." The cashmere suit was the last word in male fashion, as were "sportsman" shirts and "Chicago" footwear. "Murray & Latman" was the most recherché toilet water. Cigarettes of assorted brands, and vaseline and quinine water for hair care, were consumed in quantity. Hotels developed as cities grew, especially in San Juan,

Ponce, and Mayagüez. Summer resorts proliferated, the favored one being the Baños de Coamo.

San Juan began sprawling out into slums and there, as well as in Ponce and in other towns, juvenile delinquency and begging became part of the scene. By 1892 the drug problem was added and prostitution was on the rise in San Juan, Ponce, and Mayagüez. The contradiction between the improving, varied life of the ruling classes and the misery, hunger, poverty, and unemployment of workers and *campesinos* became obvious. The social and intellectual life of most of the population was as poverty stricken as its economic life. Alongside the opulent bureaucrats, politicians, businessmen, and intellectuals—what were then known as "the comfortably off"—the people were mired in disease and limitations of every sort. The work day was sunrise to sunset; the wage barely enough for subsistence. The diet: for the body, scanty and of little nutritional value; for the mind: ephemeral. Clothing: shirt and pants for men, a muslin dress for women. Shoes: who had any?

In this sub-human condition the people were described by the Creole elite as "docile and lazy." They were seen as a "mass that vegetates without ideals or spiritual aspirations, devoid of patriotism, morality, and the ability to sacrifice or progress." Practicing all kinds of magic, they were easy prey for every kind of herbalist and charlatan. Living far from the city, they sought an outlet to their misery in gambling, drink, and superstition. As well respected a newspaper editor as Mariano Abril wrote: "In the Puerto Rican countryside a deep sadness reigns, reflected in the vague melancholy of the people's songs, a sort of nostalgia for a pleasanter, happier, and freer life."

Cruz Monclova reminds us how this sad end-of-the-century situation was interpreted as "the habit of submission to the colonial system," which for the leaders of that time represented "the footprint of meekness" and "loss of dignity." Juan Morell Campos saw the country as lost, and Tomás Carrión Maduro wrote: "There is no redemption, my friends, no redemption! . . . The colonial inheritance weighs on our people with the heaviness of death." [11]

The Literature of Docility

The literature on the theme of Puerto Rican "docility" has emerged in periods of crisis, when our collective life suffered from hunger, political subordination, and colonial pessimism. Our isolation from the world has made us try to idealize our real situation as a formula of escape. The educated classes have been the most guilty of portraying the Puerto Rican as subordinate to nature and the soil, thus glorifying determinism in all its phases—natural, biological, social, psychological, and political.

It is in José Gautier Benítez (1848–1880) that we meet the first manifestation of this attitude. Regarded by many as our national poet, he was both the product of a "bitter colonial experience" [12] and of the romantic tendencies of his period, "one, aristocratic and feudal . . . ; the other, petty bourgeois, revolutionary in appearance but utopian and conservative in reality . . ." [13] Thus in his poetry the utopian gives place to the unreal:

> All that is in you is voluptuous and light
> Sweet, gentle, caressing and tender,
> And your moral world owes its enchantment
> To the sweet influence of your external world.

So, too, the struggle to free the Negro is deformed into a conservative concept which hides all the historical drama:

> when the yoke of the captive was destroyed . . .
> we saw Redemption without Calvary.

All of Gautier Benítez' poetry is oriented toward the soft, the sweet. Utopianism determines the patriotic sentiment, but then denies the reality of a society submitted to the feudal exploitation of a decadent European monarch.

From Gautier Benítez' romantic-aristocratic-feudal leanings we proceed to the petty bourgeois, seemingly revolutionary attitude of Luis Muñoz Rivera (1859–1916). Honored by the colonial government through its Department of Public Instruction and the Institute of Puerto Rican Culture, Muñoz Rivera displays his pseudo-revolutionary stance in what his biographers and defenders have called his "pragmatic politics." Behind this phrase is concealed the lack of faith in the people that characterized his life, a lack of faith which was, as Aníbal Ponce has said, "the emphatic affirmation of the man who thinks over the man who lives; the scorn for struggle and action; the arrogance of the intellectual elite with their proud conviction that, outside of their world, there is nothing but agitation without importance." [14] Here is Muñoz Rivera the revolutionary expressing himself in a newspaper article entitled "The Insult" in 1892:

> Thus they repay our four centuries of *loyalty;* thus they respond to our *meekness* and provoke our anger. With Cuba, which can launch its brave *macheteros* into the virgin forest and offer itself to the North American Union, it is one thing. With Puerto Rico, which has never denied its *affection* for the motherland [Spain], it is the traditional ten of the best with the lash. For Puerto Rico's history is not stained with bloodshed and violence [does he forget that the *Grito de Lares* occurred in 1868, and that 1887 was the terrible year of the *componte?*]; Puerto Rico *never unfurled* the banner of rebellion. What bitter irony! The Cubans, who ask with catapults in their hands, are thrown

a crust of bread. The Puerto Ricans, who come with humble petitions rather than taking to the woods, are scorned and slapped.[15] *

All this to propose nonparticipation in the forthcoming elections.

In his poetry, Muñoz Rivera's conception of the people comes out more clearly. He writes of the people in his *Retamas* (1897):

> Decadence is coming,
> You can feel it already:
> The once-proud people
> Has degenerated.
>
> Don't you feel on your withered brow
> The accursed footprint
> That the idea left at parting?
> This people doesn't want to save itself.
>
> If it calls, if it dies,
> It's that it longs to fall and die.

In the poem *Paris* he expresses his humanist credo, similar to that of Erasmus' in *The Praise of Folly:* "True prudence for a mortal consists in correctly judging the dose of wisdom compatible with *human nature, and dissembling his sentiments about the errors of the multitude,* if he cannot share them." What seems to be a song to the people is a rejection of the people who might threaten ruling-class stability and peaceful transition from bureaucratic colonial power:

> I condemn revolt; yes, I condemn
> Unbridled rebellion
> Which kills and robs, burns and annihilates:

---

* We emphasize certain of Muñoz Rivera's words because they illustrate the idea this "apostle" had of the Puerto Rican people and of the meaning of autonomy.

> I know that men abandon reason
> When they learn to fight
> From behind a rough barricade.

Again, in the poem *El Paso del Déspota,* in which the terrible year of 1887 and the excesses of General Palacios are referred to, the people are a "poor acacia which bends in the storm." In *Nulla Est Redemptio* they are a "humble and meek" creature who "lovingly kisses his chains . . ." And in his testament, *Minha Terra,* his whole ideology is reflected in the position of the petty bourgeoisie under Spanish domination:

> Puerto Rico, you pallid Puerto Rico
> You cannot break out of your jail,
> Because you lack—long live Christ!—
> Much nerve in your character,
> Much lead in your hills,
> And much steel in your valleys;
> Because in your fields there is no people;
> Because in your veins there is no blood.

With the depression of 1929, in a climate of discontent and social deterioration and under the influence of nationalism though not linked to it, there arose a movement described in our literature as the "generation of the 30's." A new generation of intellectual youth called for an examination of conscience; they wanted answers in order to find their identity. They were concerned with two key questions: Who are we? Why are we? It was a generation with the courage to set down its preoccupations in black and white. Its greatest mistake was seeking our roots not in the people themselves but in Spain: it suffered under the same difficulties as the Spanish generation of 1898, with its fragmentary and partial interpretation of the world and of the Puerto Rican. Its chief tendency was the Hispanic one of abstract creation, and in the words of Margot Arce de Vázquez, "Hispanism . . . is a reflexive mood of patriotism" for those who "deny that economic liberation and social security programs are enough; also, and above all, the spirit must be liberated." [16]

This generation marched beside other great ideological movements, distinguishing between spirit and matter and seeking liberation in a "Puerto Rican affirmation" which could not be proclaimed behind the people's backs. It expressed itself in the journals *Isla, Indice,* and *Brújula,* and had Antonio S. Pedreira as its ideological mentor and his *Insularismo* as its bible. Its guilt before history was propagandizing for a whole determinist interpretation which weighed like lead upon later generations.* It saw Puerto Rico as a "hodgepodge" with gloom as part of our personality: the "landscape" had helped shape our character as a people, our geography was "soft" and "feminine."

Ideology is a combination of theory, system, at times simply state-of-mind, forming a whole: "An ideology necessarily includes feelings, sympathies, antipathies, hopes, fears, etc." [17] Within this aggregation we can observe the

---

* To justify ruling-class ideology, determinism was developed into a science, a metaphysical doctrine which made all phenomena conditional on the circumstances in which they were produced. Theoreticians and scientists sought to explain a world where the individual or the collective is conditioned by geography, by race, by economic, social, or political development. Thus they defended exploitation on the basis of social Darwinism and established racial categories of backward or "underdeveloped" peoples, with race or geography determining national character, and even behavior. At the beginning of the twentieth century this was called the "white man's burden," and imperialism hid itself behind the mask of a "civilizing" mission. This mission was supposed to bring the benefits of Western, Christian civilization to subject peoples. A whole theory of the Nordic peoples' superiority over tropical peoples emerged, and a whole system of colonialist exploitation based on Christian ethics was developed.

feelings of a class, the antipathies and hopes and fears of a class. And thus we will find the ideology of the dominator and dominated, the exploiter and exploited, the colonizer and the colonized.

But in studying the Puerto Rican character we cannot take off from only *one* typical idea. As Richard Levins says, "Puerto Rican political ideology is not uniform in all its sectors. Nor is it something homogeneous . . . For us, national character is a set of ideas, contradictions, and their interrelations." [18] We cannot accept as our heritage from this generation that consumed itself in its own "creative fire" the determinism of many of its ideas, the error of many of its concepts of man, the soil, history, and struggle as the process of liberation.

And while the chief aim of these writers of the 1930's was to rescue the mind of a community damaged by colonialism through certain Hispanic—and purportedly universal—values (hence their need to examine their own consciences in order to assert themselves), their social aggressiveness was no more than a leaning toward a timid agrarian reform which fell far short of the militant agrarianism of the Mexicans. Their *independentismo* spirit fed on a utopian socialism which made them first cousins of the autonomists. Their political affiliations, with some exceptions, remained within the limits of the traditional parties. They saw some hope in the *jíbaro*, but their fatalistic vision made their view of him incorrigibly romantic. Antonio S. Pedreira's *Insularismo*, Manuel Méndez Ballester's *Tiempo Muerto*, Enrique Laguerre's *La Llamarada*, and Vicente Géigel Polanco's *El Despertar de un Pueblo* are the works of a generation within a particular historical framework. They are the products of *one* conception of man, the land, and history.

When we seek an explanation of the attitudes of the Puerto Rican of this period, when we try to understand his answers to the questions "Who are we?" "Why are we?" we come upon *Insularismo*. This interpretive essay on our reality contains influences of all the determinist theories fashionable when it was written in 1934. No other book has had such repercussions among Puerto Rican intellectuals or enjoyed more popularity and publicity. Thus a whole series of misconceptions has been transmitted from generation to generation, without their harmfulness ever being categorically challenged. Pedreira is hoping to find a definition of our reality by means of a regional analysis. His aim, he says, is "to point out the disparate elements that can make sense of our personality." So he plunges in and finds that the mixture of races creates a confusion in our character—and that "our rebellions are momentary, our docility permanent." The climate "melts our will" and makes us *"aplatanados."* * Our history is that of a "rudderless ship" vacillating between incompetence and fear. Absence of originality is a feature of our character, and rhetorical pill-gilding is a national disease which no one of us escapes.

Why did *Insularismo* become the book of the hour? Why the popularity of Pedreira's definition of the Puerto Rican? To understand, one has to see Pedreira as only one of several exponents of the literature of docility. The definition of our character he produced was adapted to the interests of the ruling class; its view of our people followed the current of the end-of-nineteenth-century intellectuals and was cut to the measure of the "pragmatic politicians." Above all it was a justification of the colonialism to which we have been submitted, for the racial and geographical premises on which Pedreira relies to define the Puerto Rican's character have been discredited by the history of humanity in recent decades. Examples are the Africans'

---

* *aplatanados:* an indigenous peasant word implying a lack of strength, spirit, or the will to resist.

fight for independence; the establishment in the Americas of the first socialist state, Cuba; and the continuing resistance of the Vietnamese people to North American aggression.*

The "literature of docility" did not die with the generation of the 1930's. In 1962, René Marqués published "El Puertorriqueño Dócil," an explanation of the failure of the nationalist movement of the 1950's which reflected the pessimism of the intellectual elite of that decade.† Marqués defines himself as both pro-independence and pessimistic, as Puerto Rican and docile. He re-masticates the pseudo-scientific hash of Pedreira, but what Pedreira sees as geographical factors, Marqués sees as psychological. His theory of "docility" denoted only an aristocratic attitude which brought the writer's class prejudices and fear of the people to the surface. To prove the Puerto Rican's docility Marqués took contemporary literature "as a springboard for the examination of psychological realities." He had previously explained the docility *à la* Pedreira as an "historical inheritance": "Puerto Rico was

---

* Another source of justification for the colonial situation came from José Colombán Rosario, a self-styled sociologist who in 1935 insisted on defining the *jíbaro* in the same terms which Pedreira had defined the Puerto Rican. For Colombán Rosario the *jíbaro* was "suitable material to be guided by a *cacique*." He was lazy, weak, and characteristically spiritless, and his docility could be counted on. See Colombán Rosario, *Desarollo del Jíbaro de Puerto Rico y su Actitud Presente Hacia la Sociedad* (San Juan: Bureau of Supplies, Printing & Transportation, 1935).

† The Ateneo Puertorriqueño awarded the book a prize in 1960, and the author read parts of it before the Sixth Congress of Puerto Rican Psychologists on August 26, 1961, at the University of Puerto Rico. Mexico's *Cuadernos Americanos* reproduced it in 1962 and the University of Puerto Rico's *Revista de Ciencias Sociales* in 1963. See René Marqués, *Ensayos, 1953–1966* (San Juan: Ediciones Antillana, 1967).

colonized by a handful of faintly industrious or frankly lazy people who had learned their docility in Spain, where they were of low social rank . . . With them would be fused, without much effort, two primitive ethnic groups that had been made docile by forced labor and slavery, Tainos [Indians] and Africans." [19]

Marqués aimed to show that free-state-ism was the psychological synthesis of the Puerto Rican personality, and that its two aspects, nationalism and annexationism, are characterized by a self-destructive drive. And so he submitted to us his novel "proof" of docility. One notes with interest that much of the "proof" is in his own works, his short stories, plays, prologues, essays, and novel. If we followed his "logic" we could conclude that the docile one is the author. In fact he represents the continuation of the ideology of the pseudo-scientific writers, best expressed by Pedreira: the belief in our *inability* to take action and the *lamenting* of colonial reality. Marqués' is the pessimistic ideology of a writer who has been overcome by colonialism, of which he is a part. He rigs up a theory on scholastic foundations to reach a spiritual level from which he loses sight of the economic, political, and ideological struggles raging in the heart of human societies.

As Marqués himself says, he speaks for those who "seem undisposed to let themselves be trapped in the net of a concrete ideology." We find that he is the prototype of the writer who uses the patriotic theme not to attack a system, a structure, an ideology, but to recreate a state of mind produced by assimilation into the colonial medium. He is the standard-bearer of a theory of antipathies which serves well to garner plaudits from the middle class and the bureaucrats, postulating a so-called independence which will not "trap one in the net of a concrete ideology." This position has parallels with that of the native bourgeoisies and with humanists who carry the word "democracy" in their mouths while reserving their heart's core for the aristocracy. The docile Puerto Rican is essentially a colonialist's construct based on a determinist concept.*

Thus we have two types of docility: the one that is applauded and the one that is deplored. The applauded docility serves the interests of imperialism and the ruling classes, and establishes as a "social value" an alleged characteristic which permits the exploitation of Puerto Ricans. The deplored docility, the docility of a Muñoz Rivera, is the self-justification of certain reformist positions.

---

* The weakness of our bourgeoisie toward imperialism is a fact. It arose from the class interests linking it with the North American power structure, in which it assumed the junior-partner role in exploiting the Puerto Rican masses. It responded to a phenomenon of a political, not a psychological, nature. When, however, the bourgeoisie confronted the far-from-docile workers it used violence to repress the labor movement whenever it thought it necessary.

II

Dust created by centuries, yellow dust . . .
When the pain came to cast its shadow upon you.
When the rigging of ships.
When the anchors of ships . . .
Then was Pedro's word.
For Pedro spoke, and his word,
his word was in the land . . .

Pedro was the land!
Pedro brought the blood.
Man died for the land.
Elías died. Hiram died. Griselio died.
And Pedro was buried.

José Manuel Torres Santiago

A New Personality in History

The worker, a new personality in Puerto Rican history, began to make his presence felt as early as the uprising of 1868, "but it was in 1898, on the very inauguration day of the autonomous government, that the working class called attention to itself. For the first time workers participated in a public ceremony with slogans of their class and marched behind the unfurled red banner." [20]

They were not the workers of the traditional political parties—of Muñoz Rivera, or of José Celso Barbosa, or even of José de Diego. They marched behind a Spanish worker with an anarcho-syndicalist background, Santiago Iglesias Pantín. Their world was not that of the lawyers, doctors, and pharmacists trained in Europe and North America, or that of the estate owners and merchants who did business with Spanish, German, Dutch, and U. S. firms operating in San Juan. It could not be: these represented the ruling classes who had joined the Spaniards in exploiting them.

Their leadership sprang from the great laboring masses who worked in cane and tobacco fields and on coffee haciendas. Oppressed by Spain and its government, they applauded its defeat by the U. S. army. Santiago Iglesias was set free from the jail in Fajardo by Gen. Nelson A. Miles' troops, who pursued the retreating Spanish. It was a time of general confusion, heightened by Miles' proclamation that: "We come in the cause of liberty, justice and humanity . . . to promote your prosperity . . . , to give to all . . . the advantages and blessings of enlightened civilization." As Tomás Blanco tells us: "Most of the popular classes, the *campesino*, the laborer, the artesan, blind to the greatness of the hour, merely reflected—they

49

were not in a condition to do more—the confusion of the upper strata. Their ingenuousness, slightly modified by the mistrust that anything foreign or strange tends to awaken in simple and good people, expressed itself in a hesitant mixture of curiosity and timidity, of passivity and the fascination of novelty. Many, by dint of hearing the conqueror and his agents say it, believed themselves truly redeemed. Finally, the confusion was compounded by a hurricane of rare violence in August 1899, which leveled the island and left a great part of the population to the invading army's charity." [21]

The evolution of our ruling class went through what has been called a liberal stage. These people formed the Liberal-Reformist Party in 1869, then appeared in an "assimilationist" party in 1883 and the Autonomist Party in 1887. In 1897 there was a split between the Liberals and the "pure" Autonomists, leading to the establishment of Muñoz Rivera's Federal Party and Barbosa's Republican Party. Personal squabbles rather than differences of ideology or program ruled the life of these parties. The emergence of the Unionist Party in 1904 brought no change in the political landscape except for the switch of Rosendo Matienzo Cintrón, disillusioned by the Republican Party, to the Unionist Party, which had an *independentista* group within it.

None of these parties in reality identified with the workers. There is nothing in the record of that "man of the people," as his biographer describes Barbosa, that shows solicitude for the workers; Muñoz Rivera never went beyond expressing his "sympathy" for them; and de Diego said that "San Juan isn't Barcelona" and the worker had to be educated before he could be exposed to "subversive" ideas. As Gordon Lewis said: "Both the Republicans and the Unionists were prepared—the first in the years after 1900, the second in the period after 1919—to collaborate with American governors for the purpose of hobbling the trade union and labor movements; and the Unionist Resident Commissioner in Washington actively helped to export the 'Red Scare' panic of postwar Republican America to the island." [22]

Thus the only movement of an ideological character at the start of the century was the workers' Socialist Party. On May 1, 1900, the first Workers Congress was held in Puerto Rico. Union membership of 5,000—which would rise to 28,000 in twenty years—was announced. In 1923 the central union body recorded an annual income of more than $10,000. Such figures show the consolidation of proletarian organizations and the growth of class consciousness and militancy among the workers. Between 1917 and 1920 the Socialist Party hailed Russia's October Revolution as an achievement of mankind and of the workers. During all this time the socialist movement, composed of *aplatanados*, "meek" and "docile" Puerto Ricans, waged a socio-political and economic fight, standing up to union bosses, Republicans, and Liberals. It fought unflinchingly against police repression. Through a broad strike movement it challenged the power structure, and it developed an extensive workers' education program in workshops and factories. The working class entered the struggle on an electoral level as well, "forming a workers' party which triumphed in the Arecibo municipality in 1914* and which constituted itself as the Socialist Party at Cayey the following year. The party received more than 24,000 votes in the 1917 elections, rising to 59,000 in 1920. The increase continued till 1936 when there were 144,000 Socialist votes. And then the crisis . . ." [23]

The crisis began in the early 1930's when the Socialist

---

* Note that this was the first time in all of America that a workers' and peasants' party had won control of an administration. The Socialist Party's error was in thinking it had come to power.

Party became corrupt, faltered, and surrendered its banner
to social reform; when the leadership fell under the influence of Samuel Gompers' American Federation of Labor;
when Santiago Iglesias converted the instrument of the
workers into his personal property; and when the party
entered a coalition with the Republicans.* It dug its own
grave when it took the road of opportunism, of surrender
to the ruling class, of betrayal. Not metaphorical betrayal,
not betrayal as an emotional epithet, but real betrayal:
surrender to the big sugar corporations.

When someone talks to us of the suicidal tendency ob-
servable in the Puerto Rican assimilationist, and especially
the black assimilationist, the simplification falls of its own
weight. Within the assimilationist point of view were various lines converging upon the same point, based not on a
"suicidal tendency" but subject to rational historical explanation. When we compare Cuba's history with Puerto
Rico's what stands out is the development of reformism in
Puerto Rico. Attempts to explain this as a psychological
phenomenon, the result of the Puerto Rican character, only
show how far the colonized writer can wander. Puerto
Ricans could arrive at assimilation through a process of
idealization, by virtue of a propaganda about the gracious
liberality and democracy of U.S. civilization which dove-
tailed into North American geopolitics. This was indeed
an idyllic and romantic vision of U.S. imperialism, but it

* The Socialists would soon leave this coalition, weakened and
divided as it was between the Bolívar Pagán and Prudencio Rivera
factions. The Popular Party took advantage of this to steal the Socialist program. The Republican Party absorbed the Socialist Party
and came to stand for annexation of Puerto Rico to the United
States and the assimilation of the Puerto Ricans into part of the
American melting pot.

was a reality for many liberals. Puerto Ricans could arrive at assimilationism in reaction to the discrimination, denial of rights, and racism which they—especially our black population—had experienced from their own ruling class. Even though this was based upon myths about the United States and ignorance of the racist foundations on which that nation was built, it is one reason for the support given by blacks to the Republican Party.

Others arrived at assimilationism by defending the class interests that were linked to big business and the banks. One study described the investment situation as follows: "Two American concerns were organized with assurances of tax concessions even before the presidential proclamation of 1901. The first was the result of a banking venture by four Boston citizens: in October 1898 they set up in Puerto Rico the firm of Ford and Co., which in the following February invested part of its capital in Hacienda Aguirre of Bahía de Jobos. This first investment was followed by acquisition of more sugarcane lands and the formation of the Sindicato de la Central Aguirre, in July 1899, with initial capital of $525,000. Large-scale operations began in 1900. In November of that year New York capital formed the South Porto Rico Sugar Co., a New Jersey corporation with $5 million capital whose big sugarmill in Guánica began grinding in 1903. A third firm incorporated on the American continent, the Fajardo Sugar Co., was formed in New York in 1905 with capital of $2 million. In 1907 the Loíza Sugar Co. was formed in Puerto Rico. Meanwhile Aguirre had converted itself into a Massachusetts trust company with $2 million capital. Not until 1926 did another sugar-investment firm arrive, the United Puerto Rican Sugar Co., which later called itself Eastern Sugar Associates." [24] Puerto Rico, which had always been a country which sold more abroad than it bought, found that by 1901, 78 percent of its products were being bought by the United States. With the decline of agricultural independence, imports of food products rose.

The cigar and cigarette industry was essentially in absentee hands; the American Tobacco Co. began to operate soon after the beginning of the U. S. regime. Coffee, our chief product under Spanish rule, fell by 20 percent in the total value of exports in 1901. In 1928 it represented only 2.5 percent of the total value of exports. This brought about the bankruptcy of our coffee economy, with the well-known displacement of men and capital into the sugar sector controlled by U. S. corporations and the elimination of many small coffee-growers.

By 1930, according to the same study quoted above, "total bank resources for the island's commercial purposes were $82 million. More than half of this amount was in the hands of the National City Bank of New York, the Royal Bank of Canada, and the Bank of Nova Scotia." [25] The rest of the bank capital was under the control of the Banco Popular, the Crédito y Ahorro Ponceño, and two new banks: the Banco de Ponce, established in 1917 by Pedro Juan Rosaly and a group of businessmen, and the Roig Commercial of Humacao. These concerns, dedicated to speculation and to controlling credit and investment, created the economic base which the annexationist movement needed to survive. They also had the official protection of a government which, in view of its ties with finance capital, found it convenient to destroy the old patterns of a small-proprietor–patriarchal economy. The capitalist revolution had started in our country.

There is no need, then, to look to an alleged docility with suicidal tendencies for the origins of the annexationist movement. They are to be found in the capitalist transformation of the means of production and consumption. Or, in Marx's words: "The need of a constantly expanding market for its products chases the bourgeoisie over the whole surface of the globe. It must nestle everywhere, settle everywhere, establish connections everywhere." [26] Feudal, patriarchal relations are thus destroyed and the road cleared for open and shameless exploitation. Professionals are converted into salaried servants. Production and social conditions are continually revolutionized. Beliefs, ideas, and relationships are broken. Our own incipient bourgeoisie was aborted and became instead the junior partner of the U. S. bourgeoisie. The subject economy grew as the new manifestation of our people's colonial subjection.

The intellectual faced with this situation can either take the side of the people—if he understands the processes that move within the people and the contradictions set up by those processes—or he can react against the people in the manner of the sixteenth-century humanists, "justifying for the bankers' and speculators' benefit the iniquitous exploitation of the masses." [27] Or he can say that the people— in this case the Puerto Ricans—are *aplatanado, ñangotado,* "resigned," "fatalistic," "pacific," "tolerant," "docile." But it is wrong by any standard to rationalize the Puerto Rican's alleged lack of self-sufficiency, belittling him because of his own impotence before his people's problem: colonialism.

North American Citizenship

The imposition of North American citizenship on Puerto   Ricans in 1917 must be understood within the framework of a military government issuing military orders. An order of February 6, 1899, issued by the military governor, Gen.

Guy V. Henry, reorganized the government, reducing it to four office secretariats, and did away with the autonomous cabinet, pronouncing it "incompatible with American methods and with progress." [28] An order of May 9, 1899, by the then military governor, Gen. George W. Davis, replaced the office secretaries with a civil secretary—a job which went to Dr. Cayetano Coll y Toste of the Republican Party.

The Foraker Act of 1900 permitted the U. S. Congress to establish a regime without authority on vital questions and created a political climate of limitations. It made commerce subject to U. S. coastal trade laws; it installed a customs system with regard to imported products and a monetary system in which the U. S. dollar became the currency of the country. All the U. S. laws which were locally applicable were to be imposed, and a judicial system whose employees and functionaries had to swear fealty to the U. S. Constitution was set up. There was also to be a Supreme Court and a federal court. The post of Resident Commissioner was instituted, and federal and military authority was established over everything not otherwise specified.

With the establishment of a legal and constitutional framework, the door was opened wide for absentee businessmen and capital to impose their economic dominion. On foundations that began to signal absentee economic penetration a political scaffolding was erected to "legalize" the system and fortify the conservative structure of parties which lacked any ideology and were guided by strictly electoral perspectives. These parties operated under a system of alliances between the top leader, the local machines, and a coalition of factions and interests. Starting with the Foraker Act and followed by the Jones Act of 1917 and Public Law 600 of 1950, which established the Free Associated State, the whole procession of laws imposed on Puerto Rico was nothing but a U. S. operation to assimilate and permanently dominate the island.*

Compulsory U. S. citizenship for Puerto Ricans was debated as early as 1900. It was opposed by Senators Henry M. Teller from Colorado, S. M. Cullon from Illinois, and J. C. Spooner from Wisconsin, who at the same time opposed statehood for the island. Teller is quoted as having said: "I don't like the Puerto Rican. They are not fighters like the Cubans. They were under Spanish tyranny for centuries without showing enough manhood to oppose it. Such a race is unworthy of citizenship." [29]

But by 1905, when American economics had progressed, Theodore Roosevelt said: "I earnestly advocate the adoption of legislation which will explicitly confer American citizenship on all citizens of Puerto Rico." [30] In the discussion of the Olmsted Bill in 1910 the possibility of imposing citizenship was again raised, and in 1912 this discussion was resumed in the U. S. Senate. On March 12, 1914, the House of Delegates, at that time the only body elected by the Puerto Rican people, sent a "Memorandum to the President and Congress of the United States," rejecting the imposition of U. S. citizenship and the elimination of Puerto Rican citizenship (which the Foraker Act of 1900 had retained): "We firmly and loyally oppose our being declared, against our express will or without our express consent, citizens of any other than our own beloved country which

---

* A long struggle was involved in this legislative process. The U. S. government sought to assimilate what we might call the "nationalist rearguard," and made concessions to Puerto Ricans to undermine the independence movement. Thus we must differentiate between the directly assimilationist laws representing the Yanqui offensive and the autonomist laws representing the Puerto Rican counteroffensive. The Free Associated State had a dual nature: on the one hand, it was a step toward statehood and a permanent union; on the other, a step toward independence because it revived the debate within our nation.

God granted to us as an inalienable gift and incoercible right . . ." [31] However, the document was distinctly timid: the major concern was the prospect of losing customs income and of having to "impose a 4 or 5 percent tax on the value of property . . ." [32]

In a speech before the U. S. Congress on May 5, 1916, Muñoz Rivera, then Resident Commissioner in Washington, said: "For sixteen years we have endured this system of government, protesting and struggling against it, with energy and without result." Of the action Congress might take, he said: "It can, by a legislative act, keep alive the hopes of the people of Porto Rico or it can deal these hopes their death blow." Faithful to the line he pursued all his life, Muñoz Rivera made this plea to the assembled Congressmen: "In Porto Rico no blood will be shed. Such a thing is impossible in an island of 3,600 square miles. Its narrow confines never permitted and never will permit armed resistance. For this very reason Porto Rico is a field of experiment unique on the globe . . . Our behavior during the past is a sufficient guaranty for our behavior in the future. Never a revolution there, in spite of our Latin blood; never an attempt to commercialize our political influence; never an attack against the majesty of law. The ever-reigning peace was not at any time disturbed by the illiterate masses, which bear their suffering with such stoic fortitude and only seek comfort in their bitter servitude, confiding in the supreme protection of God. (*Applause.*)" [33]

The Jones Act was passed, removing the last obstacle to U. S. economic penetration. The people, 60 percent illiterate, didn't understand, or didn't care, what was happening. The incapacity and vacillation of the petty bourgeoisie and the traditional parties was responsible for the imposition of U. S. citizenship—which included the obligation to serve in the U. S. armed forces. Themselves bereft of an ideology, those groups had no moral banner to raise that could have aroused the masses to militant rejection.*

In the fight against the Jones Act, José de Diego emerged from his temporizing stance toward independence to become its chief spokesman. Replying to people who muttered about our "lack of combativeness," he said: "The Puerto Ricans made a Puerto Rican revolution and helped in three Cuban revolutions. We sent two militia companies to Santo Domingo in the seventeenth century to fight the British . . . and in the nineteenth century more than 1,000 Puerto Rican soldiers fought for Cuba's freedom." [34] He stated his position bluntly: "No person of average mental capacity can fail to grasp that citizenship collectively imposed on Puerto Ricans would raise a new obstacle to the ideal of independence and to its preservation and propagation." [35]

In this spirit de Diego became a campaigner for the Caribbean ideal of a confederation. He called the Jones Act what it was—an imperialist project—and armed the Word by defending our language against U. S. plans for cultural assimilation. To those who accused him of "inconsistency" in himself accepting U. S. citizenship he replied: "If the citizenship decree had not been compulsory . . . I would have taken refuge in the maternal warmth of my own citizenship. I needed U. S. citizenship to raise my voice and fight for restoration of Puerto Rican citizenship, for the creation of our Republic . . ." [36] Thus he saw it as a fight "within the regime against the regime," in the framework of loyal opposition but with possibilities

---

* The law was so important for U. S. domination that in 1952, when the Free Associated State (Estado Libre Asociado—ELA) was introduced, it was kept along with the ELA Constitution. Thus were reserved to the U. S. government decisions that were vital to the people's sovereignty.

of greater radicalization. His death in 1918 cut short the process to which he had committed himself and left on the nationalists' shoulders the heavy weight of continuing the struggle.

De Diego represents an era, a historical task, and some contradictions. He was the first great orator of the *independentista* masses.

Nationalism: Its Faults and Virtues

The nationalist movement was organized in 1922 by José Coll Cuchi as a breakaway from the Unionist Party; it reached its peak in the 1930's under the leadership of Pedro Albizu Campos. What was this nationalism? A flagrantly destructive force, as René Marqués called it? A movement with fascist leanings, as described by Gordon Lewis? A group of assassins and madmen, as it was classified in government jargon? Or an organization of patriots who used violence as a method of fighting U. S. imperialism?

Nationalism as a political movement was characteristic of an era. Its ideology cannot be separated from its historical period or from its geographical setting. Attempts to classify it as fascist-oriented show a lack of comprehension of the historical process that brought the nationalist explosion of the 1930's. And to dismiss it as "suicidal" is to misunderstand its defensive character in the face of U. S. colonial violence.

In the twentieth century's first thirty years the United States imposed its hegemony on Latin America with the Big Stick policy, fostering the development of military castes and of dictators who governed under Washington's indulgent eye. There were interventions—with or without excuses—in Mexico, Haiti, the Dominican Republic, and Nicaragua. Only within this framework can one begin to understand the so-called nationalist phenomenon in Puerto Rico, for nationalism was the turbulent channel through which the people spoke out against their exploitation and social misery. Theirs was the first voice to make clear, through their leader, the main characteristics of the period: the economic, cultural, and political exploitation which define modern imperialism. Nationalism was the catalytic agent that would bring on a crisis in the traditional parties and in the labor movement, in frontal confrontation with the U. S. power structure.

As its ideological backbone, nationalist doctrine took the illegality of the Treaty of Paris, under which Spain had ceded Puerto Rico as war booty to the United States. Said Albizu Campos: "The treaty was not negotiated by Puerto Rican plenipotentiaries and was never submitted to our parliament for ratification. It is *null and void* as far as Puerto Rico is concerned." [37] (*My emphasis.*) Whence, then, comes the legality of the U. S. regime in the island? To the nationalists the regime was founded on force. To them "the immediate suppression of U. S. imperialism" could not be postponed; a struggle, face to face and without quarter, was on the agenda from the beginning. Not only because the system was a menace to the Puerto Rican, but because it menaced all America.

Albizu Campos was the main figure in the Nationalist Party: "From its inception, when [he] assumed the chairmanship, . . . the Nationalist Party promoted intense agitation for independence, of an extreme and radical nature, dramatically and spectacularly exhorting the country to stop all kinds of collaboration with the colonial regime, to move as soon as possible to the Constituent Assembly and proclaim the independent and sovereign Republic of

Puerto Rico." [38] To Albizu Campos, nationalism was a policy of defiance, of "courage and sacrifice," put to the test through "a very great trauma," "opening ears with gunfire" so that the dominant oligarchy—that of the United States—should "fix its attention on Puerto Rico."

In 1935 the police, the colonial regime's instrument of violence, began to repress the Nationalists. One policeman and four Nationalists were killed and forty were wounded in the first clash. The country was in a state of general agitation from October to December of that year, when the Nationalist Party held its first convention. Its demand that the United States quit Puerto Rico was a declaration of war. The bureaucratic and governing structure of the coalition parties was shattered by the Nationalist execution of island police chief E. Francis Riggs, and the murder by the police of Nationalists Hiram Rosado and Elias Beauchamp, the trial of Nationalist leaders on charges of conspiring to overthrow the government—ending with jail sentences in the federal penitentiary at Atlanta—and the police massacre of Nationalists during a parade at Ponce in 1937. All this produced one of the biggest political crises in our country since it came under U. S. domination.

After Albizu Campos was jailed for conspiring to overthrow the U. S. government, it became clear that "chiefism" was a defect of the Nationalist Party. The lack of an organized mass movement broke the momentum of the struggle and opened the door for the social and political reformism of Muñoz Marín's Popular-Democratic Party. Even so, suggestions that the defects in the Nationalist movement made it a mere "suicidal tendency" betray ignorance of the situation of the 1930's and 1940's. It was the Nationalists, along with objective political factors, who spurred the people to new triumphs in the 1930's—it does not matter that the capitalist reformism of the Popular

Democrats diluted the logical consequences of the workers' and *campesinos'* strength. In the same way, it was the Nationalists who, when they revolted in the 1950's, persuaded the U. S. government to concede the autonomist modifications of the Free Associated State.

Even the "failures" must be interpreted in the light of what they won for the people, rather than measured by idyllic and unreal standards. Recall, for example, the "failures" of Bolívar in Venezuela and of the North American rebels in the saddest moments of their revolution. Consider the "failure" of Sandino in Nicaragua, of the Spanish Republic against the Nazi-Fascist Franco forces; or the "failures" of Irish revolutionaries in their fight against the British, of the Huks in the Philippines. Or think of the Cuban revolutionaries' "failures"—as they were from a military standpoint—of March 13 and July 26 in the fight against the Batista dictatorship. Or, if one must add another to the list, think of the "failure" of Che Guevara's Bolivian guerrillas. There is a continuous thread, from the "failure" of the *comuneros* in Spain to the "failure" of our Nationalists and of Che, which gives a meaning to the Latin American revolution. Writers who try to reduce the Nationalist movement to a group of psychopaths, in contrast to the Algerian underground or the Cypriot freedom movement, are seeing history as a rudderless ship, and using a regional and myopic analysis.

In contrast to the compromising Unionists and to de Diego, who wanted Puerto Rican independence "under U. S. protectorate," the Nationalists were intransigent. Theirs was the chief ideological movement of the 1930's. Even though Rosendo Matienzo Cintrón had been the first to draw attention to economic absenteeism and its dangers, and Nemesio Canales had pinpointed the abominations of poverty with his sharp and ironic prose, it was the Nationalists who focused the spotlight on U. S. imperialism. It was the Nationalists who pointed to the danger of the U. S. military buildup in Puerto Rico and unmasked the cultural aggression of which we were—and still are—the object, showing how our culture was being downgraded. And it was the Nationalists—after Betances —who first posed the idea of the revolutionary seizure of power.

If the Nationalists erred it was in their Spanish-American view of America, a result of the heritage they received from the Hispanists who had idealized Spain's domination of Puerto Rico. For this was a fragmented and partial view of the Caribbean and America, limiting the Caribbean peoples to Ibero-Americans. Nationalism can be faulted, too, for its lack of adequate armament and organization; for the lack of discipline of many of its members; and for its tactical error in 1950 of equating the seizure of power with the capture of administrative centers, when in fact control of the technical apparatus was the key to victory:[39] "The whole arsenal of revolution—guerrilla warfare, terror, sabotage, propaganda—is directed toward taking advantage of colonialism by means of work slowdowns, boycotting imports, inciting to revolt, impeding payment of rents to foreigners, destroying foreign industrial installations and increasing by every means the *cost* of exploitation and the policy of domination . . ."[40] The Nationalists' whole strategic line affected their errors and thus the envisaged aim—to make the colony an economic burden— was never achieved.

The Nationalists conceived of patriotism as something abstract, in the area of what many have called the "politics of the heart." Their narrow positions on social problems alienated broad sectors of the population which would have identified themselves with the Nationalist line had it been aimed at the *immediate* economic problems suffered by the Puerto Rican masses. Its patriotic appeal, its concepts of individual heroism and of international solidarity, and its weakness with respect to the labor movement led many people to identify emotionally with it. But the Nationalists did not achieve the politicization which would have directed the struggle toward higher stages.

In this entire process the personality of one man—Pedro Albizu Campos—and his transformation from leader to symbol, stands out. The influence of the Nationalist Party chairman extended beyond his narrow group of followers. From jail he became a living symbol, a uniting banner, a force inspiring resistance. His name soared above the insults with which official propaganda covered it. His person achieved giant size in the face of writers paid by the State Department to belittle him. Sick, paralyzed, unable to speak, he symbolized Puerto Rico for all America, for Puerto Rico *is* Albizu Campos.

Sentenced to twelve years' imprisonment in 1937, Albizu Campos returned to Puerto Rico in 1947 to inspire the university strike of 1948. Again jailed in 1950 for the insurrection of that year, he was let out in 1953, his health precarious. His pardon was revoked when the Nationalists attacked the U. S. House of Representatives in 1954, and he was returned to jail, where he suffered three thromboses which paralyzed him and deprived him of speech. In that condition he was transferred to the Presbyterian Hospital in San Juan. There the man who had said "Patriotism is courage and sacrifice" remained the symbol of struggle for young people and for new generations. He was pardoned again in 1965 when the government knew he was near death, and he died in the same year. His funeral was the biggest demonstration of popular grief ever expressed for any Puerto Rican, and he entered the ranks of the immortals as the greatest Puerto Rican of his century. His words still echo as a political testament: "To take our country they must take our lives."

More on the Labor Movement

In tracing modern developments in any workers' movement one must, of course, start from the establishment of the first socialist state in Russia in 1917, when Marx's and Engels's doctrines became a reality under the leadership of Lenin. World War I had contributed to the ideological expansion of Marxism and to the crisis in the Second International. In 1919 two Communist groups emerged in the United States, the Communist Labor Party and the Communist Party; in 1920 they merged as the Communist Party of America. The Puerto Rican Communist Party was formed in September 1934. That was the year when Nationalists led the great sugar workers' strike in the face of the disapproval of the Federación Libre de Trabajadores (FLT)—the Free Workers Federation—controlled by the reformist Socialist Party.

César Andreu Iglesias, who was directly involved in this period of the workers' struggle, has written: "The history of the Puerto Rican labor movement has yet to be written. Present generations know nothing of the initial struggles at the end of the nineteenth century, the first ideological debates, the labor press (the pioneer *Ensayo Obrero*, the daily *Unión Obrera*, the weekly *Justicia*, the organs of various leanings in San Juan, Bayamón, Ponce, Caguas, Mayagüez, etc.), the formation of the FLT, the tobacco workers' revolutionary role, the militant agricultural strikes, the martyrs shot down by police, the evolution of the economic into the political struggle, the founding of the Socialist Party, the repercussions of the Russian Revolution of 1917 . . . The history of the working class's struggles is an arsenal of experience which living generations should know for their own ideological enrichment." [41]

It was the cane-harvest strike of 1934 that linked the Nationalists and the Communists with the labor movement. *El Imparcial* reported in big headlines that Nationalist Party activists had invaded the East. The strike marked the decline of Socialist Party leadership and discredited the FLT; it underlined the economic crisis through which the country was passing, and put Communists and Nationalists in a position to displace Socialist labor leaders.

Both Nationalists and Communists pursued sectarian policies. On the one hand, Nationalist ideology had no room for transitory measures that it considered "collaboration"; and it saw Communism as an alien tendency because of the Puerto Rican Communist Party's dependency on the United States Communist Party. For their part, the Communists, confused by the symbolism of black shirts and by the racial—Spanish-American—content of Nationalism saw it as a right-wing, fascist-oriented movement. The two concepts excluded each other. Clashes had already occurred in New York between Nationalists and Communists, and the first Nationalist casualty was at the hands of a Communist. Thus those who could have led a movement seeking new channels for its basic needs, who could have united the Nationalist patriotic struggle with the Communist class struggle, fell victims of sectarianism. The supreme opportunity—for such it was—was missed.

Yet in spite of the repression of the Nationalists and the Communists' shallow roots in the labor movement, Puerto Rican workers formed new union organizations in opposition to the FLT. Communist influence was visible in the Villa Palmeras button factory strike in 1937; in the organization of the first Truckdrivers Association Congress in San Juan in 1937; in the organization of sugar workers in the Toa Baja–Dorado–Bayamón district, and of waterfront clerks and employees; in the winning of leadership in longshoremen's unions affiliated to the dockworkers' union and the FLT; and in the victorious general strike on the waterfront which lasted forty-two days in 1938.

The struggle against the FLT, according to César Andreu Iglesias, was waged "inside and outside" the Federation. On March 31, 1940, the Confederación General de Trabajadores (CGT)—the General Confederation of Workers—was organized at a congress in San Juan which had 112 delegates from 42 unions. Its integrated leadership included such labor leaders as Licenciado Francisco Colón Gordiani, Alberto E. Sánchez, Ramón Barreto Pérez, Juan Sáez Corales, Sergio Kuinan Báez, and César Andreu Iglesias.[42] The leading participant was CGT secretary-general Sáez Corales. He stressed specifically labor interests —thus keeping the CGT out of the political struggle and giving it an economic orientation based on a false proletarian ideology. But the CGT grew until it encompassed 378 unions and by 1945 it had signed 83 collective bargaining contracts. In the two years before 1945 it led 67 strikes.

Despite this success, the CGT split in March 1945. What brought this about?

The dependence of the Puerto Rican Communist Party on the U. S. Communist Party made it an affiliate of the latter in the same pattern as the traditional Puerto Rican parties were affiliates of their U. S. counterparts. Thus Puerto Rican Communism incorporated as its own the theories of Earl Browder, and these were reflected in the labor movement and in attitudes toward the New Deal policies which Franklin D. Roosevelt's administration introduced into Puerto Rico with PRRA and PRERA. As the Communist Party itself has noted about Browder, his "central mistake . . . was his failure to distinguish between bourgeois democracy and proletarian democracy . . . In applying his opportunist theories to American history, Browder did not differentiate fundamentally between the narrow, restricted type of democracy conceived by the bourgeoisie and the broad popular democracy fought for by the proletariat." [43]

Bewitched by Browder's line, Puerto Rican Communism saw the Popular Party as part of the "transformation" then proceeding in U. S. democracy, Roosevelt's Good Neighbor Policy as an application of this democracy, and the Popularists' reformism as a "progressive" movement that had to be supported. In addition, the Communist emphasis on anti-fascist fronts in the early 1940's relegated the independence struggle to a secondary role. This mistaken analysis gave the Puerto Rican labor movement an incorrect view of reality and this in turn led to a split in the CGT in 1945 as World War II ended. Popularist reformism and U. S. imperialism had their hands free to defend their class interests against the workers. Reformism was allowed to consolidate itself in power. As in the case of the Philippines, the moment had been allowed to pass when Washington could have been forced into a compromise and a solution to the colonial question found.

With the labor movement fragmented and its leaders bureaucratized through official jobs and political patronage, the country lay open to penetration by U. S. industrial capital. The second stage of the U. S. invasion came in the 1950's with the industrialization of Puerto Rico under the Economic Development Administration, known as the Fomento Plan. Meanwhile, the Cold War made itself felt in the island with anti-communist hysteria and the application of the Taft-Hartley Act. The Union General de Traba-

jadores (UGT)—General Union of Workers—whose ef-
forts to unite labor in 1947 had only resulted in further
division, came into confrontation with the Taft-Hartley
Act. Employers, police, a board set up to examine the labor situation, company unions, and the government all
combined to compel the UGT to comply with the law's
provisions. And along with this came a new invasion as the
U. S. international unions began to organize Puerto Rican
workers.

The Communist Party thus lost its influence in the labor
movement. Persecuted and hounded into court, it plunged
into a lengthy internal debate which led to the suspension
of some members, the expulsion of others, and the inac-
tivity of many. Today the Party has no influence whatever
in Puerto Rico.

"Free State-ism"— The Popular-Democratic Party

Just as for some Puerto Ricans independence is a moral
problem, and for many assimilation is an injustice, for
others "Free State-ism" is "the psychological synthesis of
the weak, the timid, and the docile." [44] Both the first and
the last see the problem partially, showing a lack of understanding of the colonialism that was linked to postwar
capitalist expansion and that distinguishes U. S. imperialism. They are harking back to the old tunes of our "inde-
fensibility" as a people, our alleged *aplatanamiento* and
our inherent "docility." But as Fanon tells us so well: "The
entire action of these nationalist political parties during
the colonial period is action of the electoral type . . . The
national political parties never lay stress upon the neces-

sity of a trial of armed strength, for the good reason that
their objective is not the radical overthrowing of the system . . . On the specific question of violence, the elite
are ambiguous. They are violent in their words and reformist in their attitudes." [45]

Muñoz Marín's Popular-Democratic Party must be seen
as part of this pattern of behavior. With traditional party
structures destroyed,* the Nationalist Party leader in jail,
social and economic discontent prevalent and the labor
movement in an economic backwater, the Popular Democrats could begin to reap what the Nationalists had sown
in the 1930's. The difference was that the Popularists did
not stress the need for a trial of strength but had a reformist approach. Thus Muñoz Marín could declare on
January 12, 1940: "The question of political status, as far
as the Popular-Democratic Party is concerned, is not an
issue in the electoral campaign." And, following this line
of thought: "The Popular-Democratic Party . . . favors
Jeffersonian democracy . . ." [46] We agree with Eduardo
Seda that: "This definition means . . . pasting together
the support of the largest possible number of interest
groups to constitute an electoral majority." Once this coalition of interests is achieved and power won, everything
is conditional upon an "electoral definition of reality." This
leads to another situation: the party achieving the coalition
of interests has to avoid *any* ideological commitment tend-
ing to affect the majority combination that put it in power.

Clearly, the process responds to logical causes and not
to psychological formulations. Shelving the ideological
problem, the Popular-Democratic Party set up a balance

---

* By 1940 the Liberal Party had been split by Muñoz Marín,
the Republican Party had been divided into the Miguel Angel
García-Méndez and the Martínez Nadal factions, and the Socialist
Party into the Prudencio Rivera Martínez and Bolívar Pagán factions.

which neutralized *independentistas* and deceived organized labor. It took as its main point the land question that had so concerned the generation of the 1930's, initiated agrarian reform, and began implementing the 500-acres law. It launched an experiment in state capitalism which many confused with socialism, and pushed lawsuits against the large American corporations and the Puerto Rico Telephone Co., a subsidiary of International Telephone & Telegraph.

But by 1944 agrarian reform had in effect been abandoned: it was reduced to the establishment of a paternalistic administrative system in place of the old relations of social behavior. The lawsuits against the corporations were pigeonholed, and social corruption sprouted: "Medical, hospital and other public services, school busing, aid to the needy including the $7.50 monthly public welfare payments, food supplements, clothing and shoe distributions in school commissaries, social security, even the administration of justice, put large credits into the hands of representatives of the State . . . Thus human rights and opportunities, which had unquestionably increased since the Popular Party took power in 1940, become sources of bribery and corruption . . ." [47]

This situation created and developed political machines which established alliances with the Party leadership and determined the Party's political line. The state-capitalist experiment was abandoned with the sale of the paper, cement, and glass industries on easy payment terms to Puerto Rican capitalist Luis A. Ferré. And on the question of independence, Vicente Géigel Polanco and Muñoz Marín—in a resolution they presented to the 1944 Popular Party convention—stressed the "solemn commitment" not to raise the question of Puerto Rico's political status in the general elections of that year. [48]

By 1945 the opening to the right had become definitive.

On February 10, 1946, the Popular Party broke with the Congreso Pro Independencia (CPI), a non-partisan group organized to mobilize public support for independence.[*] In May Ernesto Ramos Antonini, following the Popular Party line, split the CGT down the middle. By the end of 1946, the coalition of interests that was to characterize the Popular Party had consolidated its power.

Who would now guide the Party's reformist policies— in a colonial framework oriented toward the United States? Roberto Sánchez Vilella, graduate civil engineer from the University of Ohio, would take charge of Transportation; Rafael Picó, Ph.D. graduate in geography from Clark University, Massachusetts, would take the Land Authority and then the Planning Board. Antonio Fernós-Isern, graduate physician from the University of Maryland, would become Secretary of Health and then Resident Commissioner in Washington. Jaime Benítez Rexach, who had a master's degree from Georgetown University, would be chancellor and later president of the University of Puerto Rico. Rafael Cordero would be Controller, and with these would be Luchetti, Cuevas, Fernández García, Buscaglia, and graduate pharmacist Teodoro Moscoso from the University of Michigan who would direct Fomento.

In 1948 the Popular Party congress declared: ". . . preserving the economic and fiscal relations that now exist . . . the people of Puerto Rico have the right to make

---

[*] Many Popular Party legislators and mayors supported the CPI. The first Congress was held on August 15, 1943, in San Juan's Sixto Escobar Stadium, attended by 1,800 delegates and with Juan Augusto Perea presiding. Muñoz Marín sent greetings wishing the Congress success in "expressing . . . the ideals which are unquestionably shared by most Puerto Ricans." The second Congress met on December 10, 1944, after the elections, in Hato Rey's Hipódromo Quintana. It was chaired by Gilberto Concepción de Gracia—later to become chairman of the Independence Party. The CPI was dissolved on October 27, 1946.

their own Constitution for *internal government* . . ." (*My italics.*) And Muñoz Marín told the *Diario de Puerto Rico* on January 3, 1949: "To emerge from absolute colonialism we do not need to resort to nationalism . . . [but to] seek new creative roads more in harmony with the immense fact of atomic energy and the incommensurability of the Christian attitude." Two years later, when Law 600—creating the Free Associated State—was being discussed, he described nationalism as "youthful error." Thus political opportunism was institutionalized through the *modus vivendi.* Democracy was understood in terms of the party in power. The system was hallowed by political scientists with the ingenuous explanation of the "charismatic leader."

Popular support made a foundation on which the party could build an enormous bureaucracy, an elite of technicians, and loyal political machines. These ran smoothly in a climate of colonial peace, with the unlimited credit and foreign investments that identified the system as a colonial experiment tied to U. S. capitalism and totally subordinated to absentee capital. The Free Associated State was the product of the penetration of foreign capital into our economy. The structure was maintained in intimate relationship with the United States' own development and its plans for penetrating Latin America.

Appraising the Popular Party, Luis Nieves Falcón wrote: "The leadership, which began as a living part of the reality of the people, lost contact with the people who gave life to the party, who made it grow and nourished it with their genius. Shutting themselves in an ivory tower, the leaders preferred to get a diluted, statistical view of the people through bureaucrats and technicians who thought in terms of 'foolproof' schemes and forgot the human element. The average became the norm, and basic needs went unnoticed." [49]

Three events ushered in the next decade: the founding

of the Puerto Rican Independence Party in 1946, the University of Puerto Rico student strike in 1948, and the Nationalist revolt in 1950.

The Loyal Opposition: "In Peace and Friendship"

The activity of the Congreso Pro Independencia over the whole island, its repudiation by the Popular Party in 1946, and the return of war veterans fed up with military service laid the foundations on which the Partido Independentista Puertorriqueño (PIP)—the Puerto Rican Independence Party—was organized at Bayamón on October 20, 1946. Albizu Campos returned in 1947 from his ten years in the penitentiary in Atlanta and contributed to the prevailing climate of agitation. His enforced ten-year absence had entrenched his leadership. The student organizations claimed him and proclaimed him "maestro."

In April 1948 a university strike erupted after Rector Jaime Benítez acted to curb the powers of the general student council. An impasse had arisen between students and rector regarding the program of university improvements which the council had submitted. The decisive spark was the expulsion by university authorities of a group of students who had raised the Puerto Rican flag on the campus as a welcoming tribute to Albizu Campos. The clash with the university authorities, and the Popularist government's support of Benítez's arbitrary measures, brought the students into direct confrontation with the system.

Violating university autonomy, the government seized the campus and hundreds of students were beaten and jailed. Expulsions and suspensions continued day after day. The whole weight of the administrative-government bureaucracy, as well as police repression, fell on the students. With the help of the people, who contributed funds, the strike went on for months. The government used all its power and that of the local political machines to put pressure on the students' families, and the student movement collapsed, leaving no trace of democracy at the University of Puerto Rico. Naked dictatorial authority was imposed; student representation on university administrative organs was eliminated, as was the student council. The tradition of university struggle was broken. The university was now subject to the absolute will of the rector, who defined it as a "Casa de Estudios" where the student came to study, the professor to teach, and the administrator to administer. For the next eight years it was ruled like a feudal estate by Benítez Rexach.

Silence, imposed by persecution and club, continued until 1956 when a new student generation gathered up the banner and resumed the struggle. The strike was lost not for lack of militancy or of support but because the class that could have tilted the balance, the workers' movement, was too divided to play its essential role. The students were, however, an agitational factor aiding the electoral possibilities of the Independence Party. They gave it the mystique necessary to recruit members, and the first organization it had. In the 1948 elections PIP rolled up 65,351 votes, surpassing both the Socialist and Reformist* parties.

Then, on October 30, 1950, the country was shaken by the Nationalist revolt. Three hundred Nationalists took part. The National Guard was mobilized and 272 officers and 4,017 men were put on active duty, with four fighter planes as aerial support.[50] Battles were fought at Santurce,

---

* The new name for the old Liberal Party.

Barrio Obrero, Jayuya, Arecibo, Utuado, and elsewhere. The Nationalists' most spectacular attack was against Governor Muñoz Marín's residence, where five Nationalists were killed. The police, reinforced by the National Guard, took Jayuya by storm after it was bombarded. In Utuado, Nationalist prisoners were executed on the street. Raids and arrests throughout the country jammed the jails with more than 3,000 prisoners. The "gag law," * was used and more persons were tried and found guilty of quoting from Betances and José Martí. Mere possession of the Puerto Rican flag was deemed a crime. On November 1 of the same year an attempt was made on the life of U. S. President Harry S. Truman. It failed and a Nationalist was killed.

The Nationalist revolt and the *atentado* against Truman called the world's attention to the colonial situation in Puerto Rico. With the postwar anti-colonial revolution flaming up everywhere, the United States enacted Law 600, conceding the limited reforms that would take shape as the Free Associated State. But, as Richard Levins says, "even the concept of victory and defeat must be seen in relative terms, and we can recognize victories in defeats and defeats in victories. Consider, for example, the approval of the Free Associated State. Was this a victory or a defeat? Undoubtedly in the short term it was a defeat, since once again Muñoz won the people's endorsement, the vote seemed like acceptance of the colony and sowed illusions about the nature of imperialism. But in the long term we can see ELA not as Washington's preference but as its reply to Puerto Rican nationalism." [51]

---

* Law 53—the "gag law"—had been inspired by the university strike and approved in 1947. Actually, it was a copy of the Smith Act and was designed to repress the *independentista* movement. The writer José Enamorado Cuesta and the poet Francisco Matos Paoli were jailed under its provisions.

What was the role of PIP in all this? In connection with the 1950 events, PIP offered only its "deepest respect . . . to those compatriots who have offered and are offering their lives for the cause of Puerto Rico's independence." In 1951, when the Constituent Assembly was called in accordance with Law 600, PIP did not participate —it had opposed the law when it was approved. In 1952 it declared its intention of winning independence "in terms of friendship with the United States . . ." The words "peace" and "friendship," which would now characterize the party's line, were stressed at public meetings.

Elections in 1952 brought PIP 126,228 votes, eliminating the Socialists as a party of importance and leaving the Republican Party—now called the Statehood Republican Party—in third place with 85,591 votes. PIP was down to 86,000 votes in 1956 and 26,000 in 1960, losing its place on the ballot. By a maneuver of the government the party was on the ballot again in 1964, but it received only 22,000 votes and was again eliminated.

What happened to PIP has to be seen within the framework in which the party was conceived—as a bourgeois party, mainly representing the petty bourgeoisie. PIP had a popular base that was essentially anti-government, but gave it no ideological cohesion. Considering themselves inheritors of the José de Diego fighting tradition, they envisaged the struggle as within the regime and against the regime, on the theory that independence could be won in "peace and friendship" with the United States. This hypothesis left out the problem of Puerto Rico's colonial domination based on an imperialist situation: it was a legal and abstract concept built on moral foundations. Faced with violence, PIP's petty bourgeois ideology made it withdraw to a position of "colonial respectability," ending up in the role of loyal opposition to the capitalist system and to U. S. international policy.

Offers from the Popularists lured PIP into playing the game of the traditional parties, and it offered no alternatives to the industrial capitalism which foreign investments were developing. Its moral pronouncements on Papal encyclicals, uttered in a Christian rhetoric, offered no alternatives to the masses. Thus the party became a disillusionment to *campesinos*, workers, and students, identifying itself with local machines and discredited leaders who sought refuge in it after losing official favor.

Faced with the Korean War and compulsory military service, the party assumed a timid posture, hoping in accordance with its loyal opposition role to win respectability in Washington. Faced with the Popular Party's opening to the right, and with the McCarthy persecution, PIP immobilized itself ideologically. It gave its time to legislative labors which were enshrined in the daily record, to speeches for posterity about reforms to the system which the system itself absorbed and made its own.

Corruption raised its head in the struggle for seats as senators and representatives: instead of making the legislature a sounding-board to discredit the system, PIP compromised with the system. The budget allocated to minority parties was used to develop a bureaucracy based on back-scratching and political favors. The party lost the mystique that had distinguished it in its first years, and every attempt at renovation and change was squelched as "anti-leadership." The struggle was envisaged on the level not of the people but of instruments of government. There was no collective leadership, no internal criticism, no education of political cadres or of the people. After its first effort, the party abandoned directed propaganda to concern itself with propaganda on a commercial basis, using the electoral process and—from the point of view of economic development—only consolidating the Popular-Democratic Party's power.

While the governing party consolidated itself, the assimilationists—the Statehood Republican Party—grew in strength and numbers. Concession of statehood to Hawaii and Alaska had a decisive influence, but the assimilationist position must not be seen merely as the result of the psychological impact of Alaskan and Hawaiian statehood. We must understand it in light of the growth of the economic structure, which permitted assimilationism to broaden its base; and also of the permanent crisis of our educational system, which constantly contributed to the Puerto Rican's sense of inferiority; of the continuing cultural aggression made possible by our politically subordinate position; and of the fact that the people channeled their protest-vote against their economic plight through the Statehood Republican Party.

PIP's conception of the political struggle was self-limiting. Rather than a party of popular demands, it was clearly defined as an anti-Muñoz Marín party: it thus limited the problem of colonialism to a family squabble with Muñoz Marín. Muñoz was guilty, not the United States; the Popularists were the chief target, not U. S. imperialism. The important thing was the legislature, not the people; the machinery to get votes, not anti-monopolist ideology and economic resistance to finance capital.* With its liberal stance in the political arena, PIP did not understand the development of capitalism as a system; it decided it was above the class struggle, as if independence could be won without affecting specific interests. Thus the party will

---

* In 1969–1970 a dynamic new movement arose within PIP. It put Licenciado Rubén Berrios in as chairman and anchored pacifism and civil disobedience into its ideology. PIP came out for a socialist republic, which brought the party into confrontation with the U. S. Navy in Culebra, and the federal court sent Berrios to jail for three months for disrespect. If the so-called new PIP continues along these lines it will certainly emerge much envigorated from the November 1972 elections.

pass into history as a great disillusionment for all, even for those who, through inertia, insist on preserving it as an "instrument" of the struggle.

This state of affairs inspired political scientist Manuel Maldonado Denis to remark: "It seems, then, that the PIP has nothing to offer even to those who, objectively, have nothing to lose by a change." [52]

The Korean War:
The Counter-Revolutionary Army

The involvement of 43,000 Puerto Ricans in the Korean War cannot be used as evidence of our "weak and docile, anti-heroic par excellence" character.[53] We must rather see it in the light of the function of a counter-revolutionary army in a colonial structure. That function is to crush any popular rising. The duty of the counter-revolutionary army is to defend the indefensible and participate in bloody assaults against the unassailable, to serve as cannon fodder in the great powers' aggressive wars and imperialist adventures. Puerto Rico, which had contributed 65,000 men (the 65th Infantry Regiment) to World War II, suffered 3,540 wounded, missing, and dead from its Korean War contingent. The psychiatric casualties still remain to be calculated.

Along with emigration, the army has been a great safety valve for the excess population which could unbalance the system. The benefits extended to World War II veterans in the form of housing priorities, hospitalization, PX facilities, dependent allowances, etc., were an alternative the colonial system could offer the colonized poor. Army service was often a means of survival: the promise of a roof, food, and regular pay, and the possibility of rising in the social hierarchy, explain the high percentage of volunteers for the Korean War. Military service also gave birth to our small military caste, which broadened in World War II and whose ties with the Cold War and the Puerto Rican status quo were consolidated by the Korean War.*

The 65th Infantry Regiment was as much a colonial force as the mercenaries England used in India. It was in the same category as the Senegalese used by France in World War I, the Moroccans it sent to the Italian front in World War II, and the Moroccans, Senegalese, and Vietnamese it used in the war against the Viet Minh. In Indo-China, as Ho Chi Minh pointed out in 1923, "Out of 159 regiments in the French army, 10 are composed of colonial whites, i.e., semi-natives, 30 of Africans, and 39 of natives from other colonies . . ." [54] France's Foreign Legion, and the regiments that fought for Franco in the Spanish Civil War, were of the same order.

One of every 42 casualties among U. S. troops in Korea was a Puerto Rican; Puerto Rico suffered 1 casualty for each 660 of its inhabitants. The proportion of casualties is the heart of the matter. The United States suffered 1 casualty for each 1,125 inhabitants. (If these examples do not suffice, and anyone still speaks of the "special" situation with regard to Puerto Rico, consider the black regiments in the United States.) The "heroes" of colonial wars are the soldiers designated by the system for actions beyond the call of duty and courage. Many such valiant actions by Puerto Ricans were described to me by Korean War veterans at the University of Puerto Rico in 1955.

---

* From the events following the conflict—the discrediting of the Syngman Rhee regime, the military dictatorship—we can see the true face of the war that the United States fought in Korea in the name of the United Nations.

They included the burning of villages, the destruction of crops, the systematic terrorization of civilians, the mutilation of bodies, the killing of prisoners performed on the road to the rear. Not to mention the use of drugs, especially marijuana and opium. Other memorable aspects were the use of Puerto Ricans as a shield in the Panmunjom retreat and as cannon fodder at Kelly Hill—where they were court-martialed for cowardice in face of the enemy when they rebelled against their officers' flagrant misuse of the troops. Such experiences inculcated a group spirit in the 65th Regiment. But as it became clear that Puerto Ricans and blacks were united in anti-Yanqui sentiments, the 65th was dissolved in hopes that Puerto Rican and black problems might be concealed in "integrated" regiments.

The absence of militant opposition to the Korean War, and PIP's vacillating attitude toward compulsory military service, deprived Puerto Ricans of leadership in their struggle. This leadership came in the militant opposition to military service and the Vietnam war shown by the Federación de Universitarios Pro Independencia (FUPI), the Movimiento Pro Independencia (MPI), and other *independentista* groups.

The "heroic tradition" is not to be found in isolated historical events or groups, as some intellectuals seem to think, but in the whole range of situations where the people have confronted the system. Effective resistance to war and the counter-revolutionary army would come as soon as a new generation could stand up to its real enemy with an awareness of its own history.

III

For they tell us
the best life is lived in the West.
That here we have *God*,
Democracy,
the *True Freedom*.

And they pay us starvation wages;
steal our natural resources;
divide our blood among themselves
and choose the shiniest and blackest skins
to bind the book of *Constitutional Rights*.

Vicente Rodríguez Nietzsche

The Roots of Power: The Economy

One economist described the attitude of the Puerto Rican government toward the U. S. corporations: "The policy of attracting new American firms has good results from the standpoint of the Puerto Rican government. Between 1950 and 1966, 1,268 new firms were established in Puerto Rico, of which almost 70 percent were operating at the end of 1966. The income generated by these firms represented 68 percent of the total manufacturing income and almost 17 percent of all Puerto Rican income . . ." [55] The American economist Harvey Perloff studied the Puerto Rican economy and charted the path for the U. S. corporations.[56] Teodoro Moscoso, head of Fomento, was not hard to convince as to which way our economy should go.

Following the "typical" pattern of developing countries, agriculture was sacrificed to obtain rapid economic growth rates in a few years, without taking into account the social and economic upset which naturally followed. In 1955 the agricultural economy was distinguished by its multiple stratification: employees, landlords, small holders, laborers. Between 1955 and 1960 large tracts of land were turned into pasture to make a quick profit. The agricultural surpluses of the previous decade dwindled, and the effects of this were soon felt. The rural population began to move into other areas where they lacked both skills and living space; they were driven into economic dependence merely to survive. Made helpless by their needs, and dependent on political machinery to solve their most urgent problems, they were at the mercy of the economic paternalism which characterized the Popularist government. Dependency took the form of the *mantengo,** social assistance, and use of public services. (One weapon against this dependency was "going north" —emigrating.)

Industrial development was bounteously conceived. It depended on foreign investment, and, as one economist noted, "in order to attract those new manufacturing enterprises the Puerto Rican government created a generous tax exemption plan that actually permits ten, twelve, or even seventeen years of total exemption of profits, municipal, property, and income taxes for those firms." [57]

On the wage front Puerto Rico offered the attraction in 1950 of a $.40 hourly wage (in manufacturing), compared with a $1.50 average in the United States. The surplus labor force in a country with 14.8 percent unemployment was another attraction for U. S. businessmen. The dollars to be made from tax exemptions, low wages, and high unemployment added up to unprecedented profits. Between 1950 and 1966, even though 564,000 Puerto Ricans emigrated, the labor force grew from 686,000 to 778,000. As statisticians recorded the mushrooming of per capita and average incomes, the city began transforming itself into a metropolitan area. A chasm was created between urban and rural populations, whose income continued to be the lowest. As befitted a structure promoting industrialization and U. S. capital, a growing middle class made itself apparent by its manner and vision of life.

Along with this economic expansion went an increase in the working class, in government bureaucracy and technicians, and in lawyers and doctors and what are known as the "professions." This class—with its contradictory interests and its top members becoming satellites of finance capital—was halfway between the dependent bourgeoisie and the worker and *campesino* and today numbers 300,000. At the same time, the self-image of what

---

* *mantengo:* relief in the form of government surplus food.

may be called the middle class (in terms of Puerto Rican income) penetrated sections of the working class, extending the influence of the middle class.

As a result of the economic expansion, there arose within the Statehood Republican Party the contradiction between capital tied to the soil—to sugarcane—and *nouveaux riche* junior partners of the new industrial capital. This contradiction was exemplified in two men, Miguel Angel García Méndez and Luis A. Ferré.*

While the *independentistas* and assimilationists were taking refuge in a moral posture based on natural rights and Christian dogmas, the growing economic dependency narrowed the gap between Free State-ism and assimilationism.

The middle class, dependent on the system and economically committed to the status quo, was essentially conservative. Always distinguished by its fear of change, it pursued stability as an economic, and assimilation into the United States as a political, ideal. The rural middle class were proprietors, sidewalk farmers. The rural merchant was the owner of a commercial farm which he merely visited and ran through an administrator, or he was a resident farmer who used his land for dairying or raising chickens. All of these had incomes from $6,000 to $7,000 a year.

Urban areas had greater social mobility and better job opportunities. City dwellers had comparatively more hope of moving upward on the scale. In spite of this, 54 percent of the population continued living in what may be

---

* Ferré headed a faction in the Statehood Republican Party which participated in the plebiscite of 1967 under the name of Estadistas Unidos. This group organized itself as the Partido Nuevo Progresista—New Progressive Party—for the 1968 elections. The Statehood Republican Party disappeared as a political organization and NPP beat the Popular Party in those elections.

called rural areas and income differentials remained constant for more than a decade: "Income growth for all rural and rural-worker families was considerably less between 1953 and 1963 than that of all urban and urban-worker families respectively. Furthermore it must not be forgotten that rural family incomes were already the lowest in 1953." [58]

The new residents in urban areas looked like an extension of the rural poor. Despite better educational possibilities, they still suffered from chronic unemployment, which according to the government was 12 to 14 percent, although in real terms it was over 25 percent. In the San Juan metropolitan area, 7 percent unemployment was reported, but we find 12 percent of the poor residents without work. Thus we must look for the reality behind "progress" and "average" statistics—for the truth behind the abstractions. And we must recognize how the system promotes alienation of the masses through scientific manipulation of the media, aimed at averting historical awareness and the search for solutions on a class basis: "Through propaganda techniques the public relations man prettifies . . . the social system's most iniquitous aspects, and thus covetousness becomes initiative, race and class hatred become 'good taste and distinction,' the rapacity of nations becomes the defense of law and order, and imperialist actions . . . become defense of democracy." [59]

Most of the unemployed lived in moldering houses, public housing projects, or slums. Their situation made them put their hopes for mobility and progress in the ballot box. The city poor, like the rural poor, were tied to the *mantengo*. Some 100,000 Puerto Rican families were on the *mantengo*, and some 200,000 had incomes under $2,000 a year. While urban wages were higher than rural, the propaganda factor in government statistics is obvious. Aware of his economic dependence on the system, the poor man of the city became a wary fellow. The worker saw his job as closely tied to U. S. enterprises. It came from an external source personified by supervisors, managers, and foremen.

The structure of domination was a mixture of political and economic interests. Quantitatively, progress could be shown in the economic (average income and hourly wage) and social (health and education) statistics, but it was abstract progress produced by U. S. investment and markets, by sacrificing control of the economy. As economists José A. Herrero and Rolando Castañeda have pointed out: "Workers' families in the rest of the island increased their incomes less than workers' families in the metropolitan area between 1953 and 1963. Although worker families in the rest of the island already had the lowest incomes in 1953 . . . public welfare benefits were concentrated in the metropolitan area where worker families' incomes increased the most . . ." And further: "The incomes that increased the least were those of families getting public assistance, mainly the unemployed, the sub-employed, and persons incapacitated for work."

In the mid-1960's the capital-intensive oil companies began establishing themselves in Puerto Rico—enterprises characterized by automation and a minimum of jobs per unit, which enabled them to oppose demands for wage increases. In addition to tax exemption and the wage differential, these companies enjoyed special oil-import quotas, and capital investment in Puerto Rico now tended to concentrate on the petro-chemical industry. "Discovery" of rich copper deposits on the island signaled another phase of economic development—exploitation of our natural resources—which would attract U. S. investors.*

---

* On February 8, 1971, the weekly *Claridad* published a confidential report of the Puerto Rican government mining commission to the effect that over 3,000 square miles and adjacent coastal waters

The system, of course, benefited families receiving income from interest, dividends, and capital gains—as opposed to low- and middle-income families.* That Puerto
Ricans should have taken refuge in camouflage or fake
stupidity is not a sign of docility. People facing the daily
question of survival develop defenses and forms of resistance against exploitation, poverty, and economic dependence. For the urban and rural poor of Puerto Rico,
camouflage and fakery and "gilding the pill" are weapons
for resisting the system.[60]

Within this expanding economy, for all the manipulation
of social and economic statistics, the new industrial society carried the seed of its own destruction. One way of
manipulating statistics is to talk of high population density,
of the number of inhabitants per square mile. But there is
no "population problem" in Puerto Rico: what we have is a
bad division of wealth, a disequilibrium between resources
and people, between natural, capital, and human resources.
The "population problem" comes from emigration into the
cities with its attendant crisis in agriculture; from satura-
tion of the cities, with their areas of decay and poverty;
from the investment of foreign capital, causing a flight of
savings that is among the world's highest; from foreign
debt (including government and individual debt) which
amounted to $1.28 billion in 1964–1965. These, along with
unemployment, health problems (in 1965 diarrhea-enter-
itis was the fourth highest cause of death), the low average

were being explored for uranium, gold, and petroleum. Among
the foreign companies involved are North American Exploration,
Oceanic Exploration, Ocean Dynamic Corp., Sun Oil Co., and
Puerto Rico Petroleum Exploration Co.

* In the early 1950's, profits on U. S. capital in Puerto Rico did
not exceed $22 million per year; by 1959 they were $83.6 million.
At the beginning of the 1960's they were $115 million and by 1966,
$281 million. See *Tesis Política MPI: Presente y Puerto Rico,* 1969.

educational level, and low wages and incomes, are the sure signs of our resource-population imbalance.

What is really threatened by our population growth—2.5 percent a year, doubling itself every twenty-eight years—is the seat of power. The ruling classes feel a mounting pressure imperiling the status quo and colonial peace. When their true enemy comes plainly into sight, the people will discover his Achilles' heel as they fight him.

The Puerto Rican School

From its beginnings the Puerto Rican school has smelled strongly of colonialism. Under Spain it was designed to create loyal subjects of the Crown. Under U. S. domination after the Spanish-American War, U. S. Commissioners set about to subordinate public education to the teaching of English. The problem degenerated to the political level when the Republicans decided to back the Commissioners' Americanization plan. Dr. Juan José Osuna indicated the extent of the problem when he wrote: "It would be very hard to specify an educational philosophy that would have served as a guideline for Puerto Rico's school system during the U. S. occupation." [61] The aims of the system, he tells us, were Americanization, extension of the educational system, and the imposition of the English language. A hard-fought battle was waged by José de Diego against the educational policy imposed under the Foraker and Jones acts, and Luis Muñiz Soufront, the president of the Puerto Rican teachers' association, has recorded the struggle of the association to keep the vernacular as the the official language of our schools.[62] Pedreira voiced the concern of the generation of the 1930's. A whole polemic developed against the Commissioners' arbitrary and colonialist approach.

Reflecting the general sentiment of Puerto Ricans in 1946, both Houses approved Project 51, which would have made Spanish the official language; acting governor Manuel A. Pérez then vetoed the bill. In April 1946 the two Houses approved the Project over the veto, and this in turn was vetoed by President Truman in October.

In 1948 the Popularist legislator Vicente Géigel Polanco presented Project 246, another language project drawn up by the Puerto Rico teachers' association, but Muñoz Marín did not back it for fear that if Washington were pressed too hard no reforms at all would be conceded. Not till 1949 was the problem of language in our schools settled—by an administrative decree from Education Commissioner Marino Villaronga.

Throughout this period educators and students fought against an unnatural and anti-pedagogic system, the main purpose of which was to destroy the Puerto Rican nationality through education. Credit for the final victory belonged not to the Popular Party, with its compromising position, but to the uncompromising struggle of the people in defense of their own language. The students, led by the student body of the Central High School, won a parallel victory when they called a strike which won November 19, the anniversary of Puerto Rico's discovery, as a national holiday.

In 1952, the year of the Free Associated State, when urbanization and slums were advancing hand in hand with industrialization, when tourism was becoming a source of income and the agricultural crisis swelled emigration to the United States, an effort was made to formulate an educational philosophy—a philosophy to serve as guide with respect to the kind of man, of school, and of values which it proposed to develop.[63] But the attempt got lost in an argument between "Puerto Rican-ism" and "Westernism." Meanwhile a system of mass promotions was pursued to enable all school-age children to matriculate. It ran up against the contradiction between mass education and quality teaching.

Official propaganda stressed the social usefulness of school and, at the same time, the teaching of English. A new form of indoctrination took shape: the dress was different, the intention the same. History began to be falsified in courses based on the idea that history began in 1940 with Muñoz Marín's "peaceful and democratic revolution." Education Secretary Cándido Oliveras provided the definition of the philosophy of the system in the "Preamble" to the Free Associated State Constitution: it was to consider U. S. citizenship as a determining factor in our life as a people. Thus began the glorification of U. S. citizenship as a "blessing" opening the door to progress and felicity. Along with this went "loyalty to the postulates" of the U. S. Constitution and coexistence of the two great cultures, Puerto Rican and North American.[64]

The school followed the road marked for it on the North Americans' politico-economic map. Anti-*independentismo* raised its head in the form of the obligation of all who worked for the government to sign a "loyalty oath" against any external or internal enemy. English was held to be "necessary" to progress and work. The idea of Puerto Rico as a cultural "bridge" was propounded, and our island began to be developed as a base of aggression against Latin America.

The language question came up again as Spanish began to be hybridized with English words. The principle of linguistic evolution did not take into account the fact that the United States had imposed its cultural and political dominion on us. The problem was not the new words which

Spanish was bound to incorporate as a result of the "rev-olution" in industry, marketing methods, consumer habits, and promotion techniques. It was the distortion of syntax, the very construction of Spanish sentences. This is what was craftily threatened by an apparatus of semantic ma-nipulation which aimed to turn our language upside down.* In the nature of things languages evolve, but the objection was that the system produced illiterates in two languages. It was not said that there should be no new forms of expression, but that people ended up unable to express themselves well either in Spanish or in English. And since it is through his language that a person thinks, this "semi-linguistics" cramped intellectual effort and ob-structed the development of nationality while making as-similation easier. Every idea about the way things ought to be expresses a way of looking at the world, and this was reflected in the debate about the philosophy that should prevail in our schools. Each group wanted educa-tion to follow its own political line, to conform with its own position in the Puerto Rican class struggle.

In 1964 the U. S. Congress approved the creation of a "Commission on Status" to "study future relations between Puerto Rico and the United States." Three political groups —the assimilationists or annexationists, the reformist Free State-ers, and the revolutionaries or *independentistas*—set forth their views on the subject, showing their different re-actions to the problems of the Puerto Rican people, their different views of life, of the economy, and of education.

Committed as they were to the most reactionary tend-encies in the political arena, in the economic structure, and in the class struggle, the assimilationists wanted Puerto Rican culture integrated into what U. S. sociologists call

---

* We do not assume here the classical position that a nationality without its language would disappear. The Irish have almost lost their language and still continue to be a nationality.

the "melting pot." Hence their irrational advocacy of English teaching in public schools, their reveries of the Puerto Rican as a North American, their concept of education to develop "good and loyal American citizens." *

The reformists took as their credo the ELA constitutional preamble: education, and hence its philosophy, should express all the mythology of Free State-ism. They stressed the Puerto Rican's "identity" with his culture, the use of the vernacular as a medium of expression and communication, and the achievement of a civilization in harmony with the "Proposito," a plan for the elimination of poverty and unemployment on the island. A contradiction emerged in their political and economic views and in the aims to be pursued, which were based on "peace" between social classes. The philosophy was described as one of "permanent union." Most of the polemic in the debate on Puerto Rican schools came from the reformists. Their position indicated a lack of agreement among the bureaucracy, politicians, intellectuals, and technicians who composed the government.

the reformists

The *independentistas* saw Puerto Rico as a "nation," formed during Spanish colonization, which had achieved a categorical definition of its own in the nineteenth century, had demonstrated its vigor by resisting the cultural aggression of U. S. colonialism, and had clearly defined the psychology of its people in its own literature and art. But they did not succeed in formulating an educational philosophy in harmony with their own ideological pronounce-

the independentistas

---

* Recently, Governor Luis A. Ferré has talked about *"jíbaro statehood,"* apparently an evolution from the "melting pot" to the "minority group"—an idea more in harmony with the new educational tendency in the United States and with the "third road" as postulated by Education Secretary Dr. Rámon Mellado. See Mellado, *Puerto Rico y Occidente* (Río Piedras: Ediciones de la Universidad de Puerto Rico).

ments.* Approaching the essence of our school problem, they looked for its causes in semantics, in lack of communication, in methodological discrepancies, and in a lack of understanding among the persons concerned.

By U. S. order a plebiscite on Puerto Rican political status was held on July 23, 1967.† It was a sad illusion that electoral means could solve the problem. We can only tackle our problems after the problem of colonialism has been solved. That is the heart of the matter.

The urgency of educating our school-age population forced the system to "functionalize" an educational philosophy that would permit it to operate. A constitutional, legal, and regulatory framework enabled the Education Department to direct its programs and orient its curricula. This functionalization had to be highly eclectic, due to the barrage of criticism, the pressures and contradictions. The philosophy was as transitory as the incumbents of the Education Department. It was instrumented from the top down, with the Puerto Rican teaching profession nowhere to be seen: a philosophy of the moment without rudder or compass and not steering toward the future. It arose not from any consensus but from the necessities and urgencies posed by pragmatic politicians and idealistic educators.

Nevertheless, the Department achieved a few of its goals: school attendance by 85 percent of 13- to 15-year-olds and 48 percent of 16- to 18-year-olds, and a total of

---

* The only attempt we know of is in *Tesis Política del Movimiento Pro Independencia: La Hora de la Independencia,* which, however, is no more than a reaction to the traditional Education Department line, and superficial in many important aspects. See especially Chap. VII, "Reconstrucción del Patrimonio Cultural."

† Despite the large sums spent on propaganda by the government and by the factions participating, 35 percent of all registered voters and more than 50 percent of the citizens qualified to vote absented themselves from the plebiscite.

daily attenders at elementary and secondary school programs exceeding 650,000. However, school dropouts ran to some 10,000 a year. Illiteracy remained constant at 12 percent, while 30 percent of the children in rural areas, 8 percent in the cities, were getting only three hours' schooling a day.

The inequalities of the educational system were a product of class socioeconomic relations in our society. Many saw them as something natural, expressed in dropouts and retarded students, a phenomenon closely linked to health and family-income problems and the difference between rural and urban school diets. This led countless educators to call the problem unimportant, one which could be dealt with "on the march." They regarded the question of an educational philosophy as implying a moratorium in education, so that its "functionalization" was thereby justified. From the long-term viewpoint this was a mere rationalization, serving to shift the debate from the substantial to the superficial. It was an attempt to conceal the school's actual role for the Puerto Rican child: "To be effective, all education imposed by the owning classes must fulfill these three essential conditions: to destroy the remnants of any enemy tradition, to consolidate and amplify the ruling class' position as such, and to head off any possible rebellion by the ruled." [65]

A point never specifically touched on in the debate was how an educational system based on middle-class values works to suppress the aspirations of children from the poorest sectors. Working-class children are penalized for not having the value systems, attitudes, and standards of conduct which express ruling-class values. As Aníbal Ponce has said: "The pedagogic ideal, of course, cannot be the same for all. Not only do the ruling classes cultivate their own . . . , but they see to it that the working class accepts educational inequality . . . as something imposed by the nature of things against which it would be madness to rebel." [66] There is no doubt about the close relationship, in high school and university, between socioeconomic status and the student's program of studies. Furthermore, the proportion of high-school graduates proceeding to university decreases in relation to socioeconomic status.[67] The school exists to shape the student to a social order, to give him continuity in an order based on exploitation. As a ruling-class instrument it penalizes students and teachers to make them conform to an authoritarian structure. It aims to brutalize them by psychological manipulation. Thus the school stresses the "smallness" of the Puerto Rican, develops a whole theory of our "limitations" and "defenselessness." It plays down our culture in relation to the "great" and "powerful" one of the United States.

A whole literature has emerged to justify the established order: Rafael Picó's *Geografíca,* Eugenio Fernández-Méndez's *Ensayos Antropológicos,* José Luis Vivas Maldonado's *Historia de Puerto Rico,* Arturo Morales-Carrión's essays, Pedreira's *Insularismo,* Marqués' "El Puertorriqueño Dócil." * Textbooks are permeated with a determinist view of politics, geography, and economics. The aim is to underline our dependency, to create an individual who thinks and acts in terms of "permanent union." Yet despite all the aggression upon teachers and students, and although the system puts them in mutually antagonistic positions, student revolt remained latent. Strikes, uprisings, actions

---

* Picó is an ex-Popularist senator, a board member of the Banco Popular de Puerto Rico, and the author of a two-volume work on Puerto Rican geography. Vivas Maldonado is the author of a mediocre and distorted Puerto Rican history. Morales Carrión is a Popular Party member, a Puerto Rican Under-Secretary of State in the Muñoz Marín administration who was later employed by the U. S. Department of State.

against property, and so on, indicated the students' continuing confrontation with the system. Emergence in the public schools of the Federación Estudientes Pro Independencia (FEPI)—the Student Federation for Independence—in 1964 led to a more direct confrontation with the "traditional enemy" of the students—the police. FEPI brought the system's authoritarian and anti-democratic face into the light. It was seen in the suspensions, letters to parents, expulsions, and economic threats with which the system sought to break the spine of the student movement in all of Puerto Rico's high schools.

In years of struggle the salaried teachers of the system had won recognition of tenure and retirement rights and of the right to join in political activities, as well as higher pay scales. At the same time economic pressures, living costs, and unsatisfactory work conditions produced an annual loss of teachers. For 1966–1967 the net loss amounted to 1,755 out of a total of about 18,000. The teachers' confrontation with the system surfaced with the job and salary suspension of Professor Ana Mercedes Palés de Méndez in 1964 and Professor Minerva González in 1967 for political activities. In 1967 liberal Education Secretary Angel Quintero Alfaro ousted Professor José Antonio Irizarry. Meanwhile *independentista* teachers were resisting the system's arbitrary acts and political supervision, and a campaign for better pay scales was launched by the Teachers' Association—which for twenty years had been controlled by a machine close to the government.

Thus the aims of the system as seen in its educational policy came into increasingly frequent collision with both students and teachers. The aim of domination, of setting controls and achieving acceptance of the system as something natural, collided with "docile" and *"aplatanados"* students several times a year. The problem was not the lack of a rebellious spirit in the youth, but of how and by whom the rebelliousness could be channeled.*

Religion: The Opium of the Peoples

see notes *a heavy sleep*

Catholicism, Protestantism, and Spiritualism have served ruling-class ideology as soporifics for the people. As the official religion, Catholicism was a restraining wall for the Spanish regime, setting up criteria of subordination, sanctioning social stratification, condemning every rebellious act against Spain with the threat of excommunication or through pastoral letters from the bishops.† Official Catholicism earned a series of privileges that tied it to the ruling classes, to the policies of the Spanish governors and of the Crown. The Church's function was to portray the system as "God's will." In officially condemning the Lares revolutionaries, the ecclesiastical hierarchy followed the standard pattern.

When the United States took over, Catholicism lost its official privileges and the door was opened for North American missionaries to come and preach their creeds. So it is not strange that the early *independentista* movement was psychologically linked with opposition to Prot-

---

* Recently, under millionaire Luis A. Ferré's administration, with Ramón Mellado as Education Secretary, persecution of *independentista* teachers and students has intensified. In a circular to school principals Mellado instructed them to send to the Selective Service the names and addresses of students graduating from high school. A blacklist has been compiled of all teachers classified for some reason or other as "subversive."

† A circular from the Puerto Rico Episcopate on the Lares uprising in 1868 called the revolutionaries "a small deluded group" guilty of "perverted behavior" and "madness."

estantism. Many saw the secularization of society as part of the new colonialism, and this view became important in Albizu Campos' theory of patriotism. Influenced by the Irish resistance against England, Albizu depicted the struggle as one of a Catholic people against a Protestant empire. The emotional Nationalist slogans about family, nation, and religion stemmed from this. Even the Nationalist flag, the cross of Calatrava, took its inspiration from a religious military order of medieval Spain. All this helps explain the accusations that Nationalism had fascist leanings.

Under United States domination Protestantism became what Catholicism had been under the Spanish, tightening the religious bond with the missionaries' homeland. Protestantism's ideological ties with the U. S. government made it an essential link for the assimilationist movement. Separation of Church and State was a cornerstone of Protestant doctrine, based on the text: "Render unto Caesar the things that are Caesar's, unto God the things that are God's." Protestantism threw its support to the Republicans—rather than to the Socialists, who challenged the Calvinist ethic, or to the Nationalists, with their religious concept of patriotism, or to the Liberals, who talked of "independence." (There were some exceptions: Domingo Marrero, a Nationalist, was a Protestant minister.)

Not until 1948 did Protestantism break decisively with assimilationism. Martín Travieso, candidate of the reformist-statist-socialist hodgepodge, backed religious instruction in public schools. Previously, the Popular Party had embraced church-state separation; now it nominated Licenciado Hipólito Marcano, chairman of the Council of Evangelical Churches, as senatorial candidate, and Muñoz Marín publicly extolled the dean of Baptist ministers, the Reverend Angel Acevedo Ruíz. By these politically calculated maneuvers Protestantism threw its major support to the Popular Party. Protestantism, we should note, had an enormous following among the poor. Further uniting Protestantism with the system were the Independence Party's announcement in 1956—advertised in *El Mundo* and *El Imparcial*—that its program was guided by papal encyclicals, and the appearance in 1960 of the Catholic Action Party with official Catholic blessings and pastorals by Bishop Davis and Bishop Macmanus.

In its turn, Catholicism linked itself to the system by naming North Americans to its hierarchy and by increasing the number of private Catholic schools under the control of North American priests, nuns, and sisters. The private Catholic school assumed an anti-Puerto Rican role in the training of students. English was the main teaching language. Thus both religious groups became co-defenders of the established order. 5 Matthew became the justification of a state of affairs which would have to be resolved in another world.

This began to change with the *Mater et Magistra* and *Populorum Progressio* encyclicals, which oriented the Catholic Church more toward social problems. A native clergy and hierarchy emerged and the Catholic Church began making changes which have not yet been completed. Added to this is the development of a revolutionary Catholicism in Latin America, which is already having an impact on events. Partial change also came in Protestantism with the appearance of a new young generation of ministers and seminarians who began to oppose the notion of an Americanized Protestant church—as if Christ had been born in Bethlehem, Pennsylvania. The struggle within Protestantism broadened as laymen and university students entered into the debate. Equally with many young Catholics, these people questioned their church's subordination to the capitalist system and the status quo, and repudiated Puerto Rico's colonial subjection to the United States. At the present time a movement is broadening within both sects to Puerto Ricanize the church. Exemplifying the new attitudes are Catholic Msgr. Antulio Parrilla and Protestant Rev. Juan Antonio Franco.*

Women: The Double Oppression

In the earliest primitive communities we find women working on the same level with men in production, and with a pre-eminent function in social life. This is because exploitation was then unknown. Under the custom of polyandry women had the right to take several men, and since the children's paternity was uncertain the mother assumed authority over them. With the growth of agricultural surpluses, the discovery of metals, the search for new kinds of work and methods of work, and with the accumulation of wealth, man became supreme in family and social life. Private property was enthroned and woman became a victim of the system. In slave society woman was seen as property which was to produce descendants who would inherit the property of man. This system was endorsed in the Bible, which constantly refers to woman's inferiority. In Homer's poems woman is confined in the house as a weaver and preparer of food—the case of Penelope. Women did not enjoy the rights of citizenship in ancient Rome.

Christianity, which arose as a revolt against slave society, owed much of its success to women; but when it

* It is known that the Rev. Juan Antonio Franco was forced to resign his ministry for political reasons. As for Msgr. Antulio Parrilla, the Puerto Rican government has been pressing for his transfer. Parrilla's present bishopric is a tutelary one.

became the church of the ruling classes the inferiority principle was re-applied. The principle was firmly laid down by Paul in his first Epistle to the Corinthians: "The man is the head of the woman." For the Church fathers woman became again "impure," the "seductress" who tempts to sin. Woman's situation worsened in feudal society. Religion, laws, and customs made her work for nothing and surrender her body. Under the "right of the first night" the serf's wife had to pass her first married night in the feudal lord's bed. A woman had no freedom of choice in marriage—she was selected more as a matter of policy, for an alliance, than for love. Personal taste was subordinated to family interest. The Catholic Church contributed to keeping woman in subjection. St. Thomas Aquinas appraised her as "born to be under the yoke of her lord and master who, with the superiority nature gave him in everything, is destined to rule." Romance literature took on the job of glorifying an era in which woman was not only exploited but vilified. It presented a restricted world, poetically adorned with embellishments that never existed. The Code Napoléon, the basis of bourgeois legislation, imposed woman's subordinate role by civil statute.

The collapse of feudal society posed the problem of woman in concrete form, for in capitalist society she participated in the production process. As Marx wrote in *Capital*: "The labor of women and children was, therefore, the first thing sought for by capitalists who used machinery. That mighty substitute for labor and laborers was forthwith changed into a means for increasing the number of wage-laborers by enrolling, under the direct sway of capital, every member of the workman's family, without distinction of age or sex." [68] Capitalism imposed upon women a double exploitation—in the home and in the factory.

In Puerto Rico men see women as inferior beings—

and this in spite of so-called legal equality. The concept ✗
stems from an agrarian regime that is now breaking up
under the influence of a capitalist society that brings
woman into the productive process as an industrial worker.
Today women are in the majority in some professions, as
nurses, secretaries, social workers, teachers.* Other professions, however, are all but barred to women: medicine,
engineering, law. Thus we still speak of professions "for
women." Religion, ruling-class morality, and the propa- ✗
ganda media—film, radio, press, TV—are active allies
against women's liberation. Virginity remains a value in
our society and social pressure is used to punish the woman
who violates it. Divorce, too, is viewed as shocking when *D. is*
sought by a woman. Of course, these attitudes are mainly *very*
found in what we call the middle class. In the working *common*
class, prejudice disappears to the extent that women are *now—*
brought into the economic process.

Although young people have been revising many of
these "values," the father figure remains the authority in
the Puerto Rican family. Thus the woman passes from
the father's authority to that of the husband. Her role as
mother, her responsibilities in raising the children, often
prevent her from maturing intellectually. In her hands lies
chief responsibility for the children's education, yet the
father remains the source of authority and hence of punishment. To escape from the husband's authority she can
resort to divorce as a defensive weapon. It is significant
that in Puerto Rico in 1968 there were 23,000 marriages
and 18,000 divorces.

As our economy becomes more and more industrialized,
the new generations are producing a crisis in Puerto Rican
society's traditional values. The authority of the father
and the husband is being questioned; divorce is im-
pinging on the dominant *macho* role and threatening the

* In the elementary schools, 97 of every 100 teachers are women.

whole *machismo* complex. At the same time, and in spite of social pressures, the new generations are experimenting with pre-marital sex relations; engagements are losing their limited character and are being replaced by more satisfactory relationships. All this has become possible with the development of a new social base that is imposing its values, questioning established mores, and revolutionizing social relations.

In 1968 we found the following picture: in a total population of 2.7 million there were 240,000 women and 241,000 men between the ages of 16 and 24. Of the men, 15 percent were unemployed, 30 percent were at school, and 44 percent were employed; of the women, 23.7 percent were employed, 44.6 percent were occupied domestically, 26.1 percent were in school, and only 4.6 percent were unemployed. Of the total 28,000 unemployed, one-sixth were classified as heads of families.

Of 701,000 workers in 1968, 208,000 were women while 493,000 were men. Taking what the government calls the "growing sectors" of our economy, we find that in manufacturing 56,000 of the 95,000 workers employed were women. In government, there were 43,000 women out of a total of 100,000; in commercial employment, there were 25,000 women out of a total of 84,000. The smallest number of women were employed in construction, with a total of only 1,000 women out of 70,000.

Since manufacturing is the largest sector of our economy, it is instructive to note the importance of the factory in women's emancipation. The factory broke the confinement of woman and buried the belief that she "belongs in the home." It also destroyed the traditional structure of the family by undermining the dogma of the male's authority over the female. It made woman economically independent of man and brought her into the economic and political struggles.

Because of their reserved attitude toward change, women have been accused of being reformist and conservative. Yet the experiences of Cuba and Vietnam have shown how revolutionary women can be. In Puerto Rico, the women's activity against compulsory military service has firmly established their importance in the struggle. Until now male control has been the chief characteristic of Puerto Rican politics, but the development of a new social base—the industrial working class—suggests that this male monopoly will be threatened by women as has happened on other fronts.

Neither feminism nor the moralization of many intellectuals has fully explained the problem of women's exploitation. The rupture of the old society has brought women into public life. The capitalist process has "liberated" women from old forms of exploitation but has submitted them to the new exploitation of wage labor. For in our colonial situation, if the Puerto Rican male worker receives one-third of his U. S. equivalent's wage for the same work, the Puerto Rican female worker receives even less. In addition, all the propaganda of the system is angled toward extending consumption and credit to create in women the illusion that they can liberate themselves through their wages.

Puerto Rican sociologists and intellectuals who are immersed in "North American sociology" have failed to grasp the nature of our women's liberation movement. The more "progressive" they claim to be, the more they stress "womanly weakness" and the more they dream of feudal, reactionary *machismo*. But women should not be seen either as rivals, or as "weak," or as creatures for the pleasure of other creatures. Women should be understood as *compañeras* who are exploited at work and at home. Only thus will we understand divorce as a defensive weapon, the miniskirt as an aggressive fashion, and prostitution as an economic phenomenon. The attitude of some belittlers of woman's role in the political, economic, and social struggle shows what primitive minds some self-styled *independentistas* still have.

If traditional *independentismo* insists on flying the reactionary banner of Puerto Rican *machismo* against the conquests women have achieved—if it compulsively insists on male supremacy—it is for real revolutionaries to light the road to woman's emancipation from her double exploitation.* In struggles throughout the world—revolutions, insurrections, protests, strikes, uprisings, and student demonstrations—woman has played an outstanding role. Puerto Rico has *not* been the exception. Since Lares (to take an arbitrary starting point) and through a century of struggle she has been in the front lines. Her role will be more important every day.

---

* In September 1970 one of the women leaders of the Young Lords accused *independentista* leaders of preventing her participation in the Grito de Lares celebration. She charged the *independentista* leadership with raising the banner of male supremacy (*machismo*).

IV

Then we will take,
though now you don't believe it,
all the dictionaries in the world
and cross out,
erase with joy
and pride
the word "boredom"
for all time . . .
Venceremos!

Iván Silén

The Search for Achilles' Heel

People who conceived of nations as homogeneous wholes, and of patriotism as the struggle of *all* classes against a common enemy, have had to do some rethinking since the Cuban Revolution. Since May 1959 the ruling classes and native bourgeoisies have been ever more closely tied to U. S. imperialism. The wars of national liberation have shown once and for all that the so-called national bourgeoisies are a counter-revolutionary element which, allied with imperialism, can drown popular victories in blood. Such has been the case in Indonesia, in India, and in the Philippines—but not in Cuba, which took the socialist road and defeated, at the Bay of Pigs, an invasion financed, organized, and inspired in the United States.

In Puerto Rico, as in Africa, Asia, and Latin America, the ruling classes are deeply involved with imperialism through technical and economic aid, military and economic programs. This interlocking runs from Point Four to the Voice of America, from the Peace Corps to the CIA. The links of the independence movement are with the masses: the workers and *campesinos* who make up the multitude of wage-earners exploited by colonialism, neo-colonialism, and imperialism. National consciousness and class consciousness are not mutually exclusive: they complement each other. They are parts of a revolutionary movement's ideology in the fight for independence and national liberation. However, the common ideology of the people may contain a form of class consciousness which is antagonistic to national consciousness. The worker or slum dweller, in class terms, can be very realistic and at the same time more pro-United States than our millionaire Luis A. Ferré. Oscar Lewis's Soledad put it this way in

La Vida: "When Tabio robbed a rich person I felt nothing but pleasure. The rich are sons of a great Whore and they take plenty away from us." And one finds the *independentista* who rejects nationalization of foreign capital and defends the North American's property in hopes of a nonviolent change in our national situation. Having only a partial view of our reality, neither has been able to pinpoint either the true enemy or the allies. Richard Levins notes six facets of this situation: progress, concern about social degeneration, democratic convictions, class consciousness, nationalism, passivity, and violence.[69] The basic discrepancy is between what is preached to us and the facts of our life. *Who* benefits from progress? *Why* does social degeneration occur? *Who* is exploiting me? *Who* is exploiting my country? And finally, *what* road do we take? It is in the answers to these questions that the synthesis between national and class consciousness is to be found.

Confrontation between official ideology and that of the revolutionary movement will bring the necessary synthesis between national and class consciousness. Often, however, revolutionary consciousness only achieves reforms or partial victories. What is decisive is the extent to which these reforms and victories contribute to the maturing of national or class consciousness, the maturing of the people's faith in their own resources and potential.* Again quoting Richard Levins: "For the young worker, injustice first appears in the form of bad luck or personal tragedy: unemployment, growing debt, the need to leave school too young or to emigrate to earn a living. Others notice first the colonial condition of their country, foreign monopoly, compulsory military service, the contempt for their culture."[70]

---

* This is to be seen in the struggle against compulsory military service and the ROTC: note how the struggle has escalated into defiance of the regime itself.

Two groups of people have primary importance in the taking of power. The first is the workers—in agriculture because they are paid least and suffer most, and in industry because they have yet to be organized into trade unions. Only 18 percent of the working class is organized. The Internationals have organized a mere 2 percent, which is exploited not only with respect to wages but by the Internationals themselves, in the form of control of local funds and rising union dues. The same fragmentation of that part of the labor movement affiliated to Puerto Rican unions has caused contradictions between organized and unorganized workers, and between the locally organized worker and the worker organized into the U. S. Internationals.*

Also to be taken into account here is the unemployed worker who is often the nucleus of the so-called *lumpen.*† The *lumpenproletariat* populate the belts of misery that surround the cities. Their activities, almost always "illicit," bring them into confrontation with the colonial regime and with official ideology. They are "the poor," the vic-

---

* Penetration by U. S. Internationals has created an additional division in the workers' ranks. Innumerable attempts by the independent unions to establish a unified center and leadership have failed. Each group has serious problems. One, ruled by nominees of the U. S. labor hierarchy, lacks union democracy; in the other fragmentation is the order of the day. Group interests and narrow economic vision prevail in both. See *Tesis Política del MPI: Presente y Puerto Rico* (1969).

† On the importance of the *lumpen,* see Fanon, *The Wretched of the Earth* (New York: Grove Press, 1963). Dr. Ana Livia Cordero, who had been to Ghana representing MPI, was one of the first to understand these people. Her group undertook a special pilot project of working in the communities with the young people of Bayamón who had left MPI after disagreements with its leaders. Ana Livia Cordero's group differed with the MPI leadership on emphasis, orientation, and style of working in these communities.

tims of every kind of restriction who evolve what anthropologists, sociologists, and educators call "the culture of poverty."

The second group of prime importance is the youth. The students increasingly speak for the masses of our population—the unemployed, the workers, the white-collar workers, the school dropouts who fill the ranks of juvenile delinquents: "The student is especially sensitive to the contradictions between words and deeds. They talk to him of liberty but advise conformity. They talk to him of the Puerto Rican miracle while a quarter of the population lives on the *mantengo*. They talk to him of freedom of the press, but what he sees is the freedom of two or three concerns to manipulate the news. They talk to him of the public employee being at the people's service, but what he sees is that the people are the bureaucrat's least concern." [71]

We must expect the maturing of consciousness to take a zig-zag line, bringing these groups by stages into confrontation with the power struggle. We know there are no magic formulas to guide an anti-colonial struggle. Victory will be won on many fronts. The conjunction of the battle of ideas with work in communities and slums and with workers, *campesinos*, and youth will lead to the higher stage of armed confrontation. This will come about in accordance with the geographical, political, economic, and social conditions of Puerto Rico.

In the 1960's the penetration of U. S. capital began to be clearly understood. Using the advantages of the colonial system, U. S. enterprises took over the Puerto Rican market. They used the superiority of their technique, efficient methods of mass production, unfair competition, control over demand and distribution and, along with these, the purchase and merging of enterprises. Thus such businesses as milk, biscuits, rum, packaging, fertilizers, ice cream, soft drinks, beer, bread, petroleum derivatives, men's clothing, printing, furniture, cigarettes, pineapple, and meat all came under U. S. monopoly control. To this must be added the control over the retail trade achieved by such chain stores as Woolworth's, Franklin's, Bellas Hess, Kresge, Grand Union, Lerner Shops, Thom McAn, Pueblo Supermarkets, Sears Roebuck, and J. C. Penney. The government developed so-called commercial centers so that these concerns had the best locations. Many small Puerto Rican retailers went bankrupt, and by the mid-1960's 80 percent of our economy was controlled by U. S. capital.

Control was also exercised in Puerto Rican purchases from the United States. As MPI noted in 1964: "The income from such purchases is spread throughout the states. The South receives $288 million, the Middle West $255 million, and the Eastern states supply $256 million worth of merchandise. Sales to Puerto Rico by California, Washington, and Oregon amount to $93 million." [72] By 1968 imports exceeded $1 billion. Profits did not come only from monopoly control of a market and of its commercial and industrial enterprises. They came also from low wages, tax exemptions of up to seventeen years on property and capital, and the protection our government and legislature afforded to a whole politico-bureaucratic structure which operated to maintain the status quo and prevent the organization of trade unions.

We were also faced with the control of the news, internationally and locally, by two news agencies. Radio, press, and TV served up what United Press International and the Associated Press wanted our people to know. The country's three dailies passed in various ways under the control of the great newspaper chains: *El Mundo* was swallowed by the Knight chain; the *San Juan Star* (read by the 60,000 North American residents in Puerto Rico) by Cowles; *El Imparcial* was taken over by Miguel Angel García Méndez, linked to the sugar interests on the island; and lastly, *El Día* belongs to the Luis A. Ferré enterprises.

All this penetration, however, made the enemy more identifiable: the more he controlled and monopolized, the greater his weakness in confrontation with the people. This then is where he can be hit, for it is his Achilles' heel. The colonized intellectual may fail to see it, but those who fight against the system—the consumer, the worker, the housewife, the student, that is to say, the people—will. The anonymous heroes of the Armed Commandos of Liberation (organized in 1969 as the fighting arm not of an organization but of the "independence struggle of Puerto Rico") are beginning to teach it to them.

Violence is the essence of a colonial society. It is established as a system in the interests of the ruling classes. Colonial society "is the meeting of two forces, opposed to each other by their very nature, which in fact owe their originality to that sort of substantification which results from and is nourished by the situation in the colonies. Their first encounter was marked by violence and their existence together . . . was carried on by dint of a great array of bayonets and cannon." [73] Puerto Rican history has been witness to this violent confrontation between people and oppressor. We see it in daily events: in schools, churches, factories, the countryside, in strikes, demonstrations, and insurrections. As soon as an individual confronts the system, he feels its violence in the way of life colonialism imposes on him: the feudal-type exploitation in the countryside, the capitalist exploitation in the cities.

The lifeblood of every colonial society is the profit it offers to its exploiters. Its basis is the authority of an exploiting system—not the authority that comes from a majority consensus, but the paternal authority with which a minority tries to justify a system beneficial to it. Around that system is built a morality, an ethic, rooted in the economic co-existence of colonizers and colonized. Thus the system envelops itself in forms that create the illusion of sharing, of a brotherhood and equality that don't exist. The Puerto Rican elections held every four years exemplify this. We must not confuse the ox with the fighting bull, the causes with the problem, the root with the branches.

The essence of the system is the dictatorship of the bourgeoisie, of capitalism and imperialism: not a problem merely of Puerto Rico, but of Latin America. Seventy years of colonialism cannot be erased with a "We are docile" formulation. Blaming our "undoubted" docility as a people cannot justify the system. We must wipe it out in the struggle, hitting the enemy and seeking his Achilles' heel, deepening our awareness that between oppressor and oppressed all is resolved *by force*.

The Enraged Generation*

The birth of the Federación de Universitarios Pro Independencia (FUPI)—the University Federation for Independence—in 1956 brought a new generation into the struggle, one destined to destroy the concepts of Messianism and patriotism which had eaten like a corrosive into the independence movement. FUPI was the chief manifestation of what was later called the "new" fight for independence. It entered Puerto Rican life at a moment of crisis, when the Independence Party suffered its greatest electoral calamity. Unentangled in the electoral sys-

---

* The original title of this chapter was "La Generación Encojonada."—Trans.

tem, FUPI moved from the mere press release and prose-lytizing assembly to confrontation with the power structure in 1960, when it challenged militarization of the university and the compulsory military service imposed through ROTC.

Its world alliances produced a break with the narrow insularism and provincial mentality of the *independentismo* of the period. The chief exponent of these views was Hugo Margenat Mediavilla, a young poet with Marxist ideas. He was ahead of his time in writing prose and verse that inspired the new generation. His posthumously published *Mundo Abierto* made him known as the "forerunner."

The new generation came to take its place in history under the positive influence of the Cuban Revolution of 1959. Marxism made its entrance on the Puerto Rican stage, with the awareness that it had overturned the theory of small countries' subordination to big ones and the imperialist-created mythology justifying colonialism.

The experience of FUPI showed the need to internationalize the Puerto Rican struggle. Some young people went abroad and felt the impact of a new world coming to birth in Africa, Asia, and Latin America. Socialism became a reality and national liberation a necessity, separated now from the Hispanic tradition that had held us back. The new generation was not hypnotized by Hispanism as the *alpha* and *omega* of all values. It matured by reading Marx, Lenin, Fidel, Che, Mao, and Fanon; and under the impact of the Cuban and Algerian revolutions and the Vietnam war. It wrote "Pedro Albizu Campos" on its banners and evolved ideologically in confrontation with the system. In that process it clarified its ideas and arrived at a class-conscious view of the struggle and the taking of power.

It developed an ethnic consciousness to put its relations

with the Caribbean, Latin America, Africa, and Asia in perspective, and realized that the struggle would be long and circuitous and impossible without understanding imperialism as a system. This brought an awareness that independence could neither be won behind the people's backs, nor be the product of an elite nor of a coup d'état, nor come on a silver platter. The struggle began to be seen as a process and a confrontation of force between imperialism and the people, and FUPI became the center for cadres who then nourished militant *independentista* organizations.*

Two parallel processes—the fragmentation and the renewal of the *independentista* forces—started in 1959 with the constitution approved by the MPI congress at Ponce. This was accompanied by the reactivation of the Nationalist Party and the rise of organizations such as United Patriotic Action, which later merged with MPI and other groups into the Socialist League.

Many have questioned whether this fragmentation was necessary. We don't see the process as negative. The various forms of work and organization have, despite their differences, led to the development and consolidation of a Puerto Rican "New Left." The determining factors were efficiency and the imperatives of struggle—to work with the people, to present a militant policy that would broaden popular awareness, to put an end to patriotic exhibitionism and liberal intolerance. The consequent revival was expressed in an examination of our reality, our potential,

---

* This was strongly indicated by the men who served as presidents: Jaime Luciaco, 1956–57; Norman Pietri, 1957–59; Juan Angel Silén, 1959–60; Pedro Baiges Chapel, 1960–61; Ramón Arbona, 1961–62; Marcos Rodríguez, 1962–63; Benjamin Ortiz Belaval, 1964–65; José Antonio Irizarry, 1965–66; Alberto Pérez Pérez, 1967–68; Florencio Merced, 1968–69.

and our forces.* Instead of the waste of forces previously characterizing the *independentista* movement, an alienating and at the same time liberating process began: an effort to build the struggle on a more positive foundation. Within MPI the conflicts and bitternesses, the patrioteering and moralizing, were soon left behind. The movement broke with pacifist tendencies and the cliché of spontaneous insurrection and the air was cleared for a new conception of the struggle, for fresh ideas of program and ideology.

However, MPI was a fusion of many tendencies, with elements from the Independence, Nationalist, and Communist parties, and from FUPI, participating in its organization. There was certainly some revolutionary infantilism in the consolidation process, some analytic confrontation between revolutionary and legal methods, and a degree of patriotic exhibitionism and intolerance in the way MPI functioned. Yet for all this we cannot minimize MPI's role in developing a New Left and a new struggle. Much of the credit for the *independentista* movement's ideological and numerical growth belonged to MPI, which in ten years of work had had to contend with the relentless persecution and repression of the system. The defects that may have existed in MPI were not the result of a hotheadedness foreign to the Puerto Rican character, as some insist. For the struggle to reach the point to which Armed Commandos of Liberation have raised it today, some cleansing and re-invigoration were inevitable.

In the words of its secretary-general, Licenciado Juan Mari Bras, MPI "is an alliance of classes, progressive ideological tendencies, and different generations. We represent national unity in embryonic form; we are the vanguard.

---

* This self-analysis produced MPI's first political thesis in 1963, the first document of an *independentista* movement ever to emerge from such an examination.

Our political and organizational progress is due to our having drawn as radical an ideological line as is feasible for a mass organization in Puerto Rico. On the day when we shift the line from that point, the vanguard will collapse. Our responsibility as leaders is to stay always on the alert, to detect where this point of reference lies at each moment. We must not drag behind it, but neither must we aim beyond it. Specifically, the point that determines our line is to be located by following the consensus of our own militants. To maintain that consensus we must take a position which balances the most advanced and the most backward sectors of the movement. The role of our young people, as vanguard of the vanguard, is not to impose their impetuosity (which it is right for them to have) on the organization as such, or to become a faction within it. Their responsibility is to help the movement's more backward sectors to mature, to set an example in discipline, work, and efficiency. Just as the movement of a guerrilla column is determined by its slowest elements, so the most backward sectors of our vanguard will determine its ideological development." [74]

The new generation is raising questions and demanding answers in the literary reviews *Guajana, Mester, Palestra,* in the Socialist League paper *El Socialista,* in *Claridad,** and in the "little press," with its profusion of bulletins and leaflets. With bonds broken and spirit liberated, the new struggle has combined an attack on social evils with calls to fight for something concrete, real, and necessary. The new generation of young writers wants commitment in words and deed. They fear neither prison nor death; they are politically involved in a revolutionary task handed down by Puerto Rican fighters of the past decade.

---

* The MPI newspaper with the highest *independentista* circulation, good printing, and dedicated personnel. It is soon to become a daily with general country-wide circulation.

The task has many facets, for in addition to being a military fortress, a monopoly market, and a source of wealth for U. S. capital, Puerto Rico is a center of operations for the Mafia—with its jewel smuggling, organized prostitution, and contraband drug traffic in the Caribbean.* The potential danger behind this is the presence of foreign gangsters and Cuban *gusanos* who, together with the CIA, could form a shock-force to be used by imperialism against the *independentista* movement.†

Organization of FEPI in 1964 advanced the goal of changing the independence movement's social composition. FEPI found the most effective means of bringing young people into confrontation with colonial authoritarianism. Its importance was clear at the Grito de Lares centenary in 1968, when thousands of intermediate- and high-school students demonstrated their solidarity and marched to Lares in tribute to the fathers of our country.

---

* Known drug addicts are officially estimated at more than 30,000, mostly between the ages of 15 and 24. The illicit drug traffic exceeds $75 million a year and is unquestionably run by the Mafia with headquarters in the United States. This means control of gambling casinos, the hotel industry, and prostitution, and reaches out into the horseracing, moneylending, real estate, and urban construction businesses. See MPI, *Presente y Puerto Rico*.

† There are more than 30,000 Cuban exiles in Puerto Rico. Financed by the CIA, they have military organizations such as Alpha 66. There are also extreme rightist elements who gravitate to the ROTC and the country's assorted anti-communist groups. These can rely on the Puerto Rican government's support and many of their "leaders" are members of Ferré's New Progressive Party. Some belong to the government bureaucracy, others—such as Senator Palerm y Misla Aldarondo of the San Juan City Assembly —to the government itself. Note that there is a close analogy between MANO and NAO, the fascist shock-forces united against the liberation movement in Guatemala, and the Puerto Rican anti-communist groups. See Eduardo Galeano, *Guatemala, Occupied Country* (New York: Monthly Review Press, 1969).

FEPI had already made its presence felt in the July 1967 demonstration against military service and the plebiscite, which was on a national scale and involved twenty-six towns. FEPI began the penetration of the slums and the gradual filling of the vacuum between the *independentista* movement and the masses. It gave young people the opportunity to "be in something": it was an expression of the ego ideal to which youngsters aspire—a natural liberating outlet against the oppressive structure.

Another feature of the new struggle was solidarity with the Vietnamese people's resistance to U. S. aggression, expressed in a boycott of the U. S. war effort and a refusal to obey the compulsory military service law. The new generation linked military-service resistance with FUPI's campaigns against militarization of the university (1959) and against the compulsory two-year ROTC courses at the University of Puerto Rico (1960). Even though the war was something 'far away, experienced chiefly through news bulletins, the Nationalist Party undertook to resist military service. Young Nationalists who refused to register with the Selective Service were the first to be jailed. On July 16, 1962, Mari Bras exposed in *El Mundo* a plan to draft FUPI and MPI leaders into the U. S. Army.

The resistance campaign began with organized refusals by draftees to swear the "loyalty oath" against any internal or external enemy of the United States. The first to do this were rejected as "a danger to national security" and classified 4F. Another tactic was for a draftee to present an affidavit that he had entered the army under protest and as a product of Puerto Rico's colonial status. José Arturo Sánchez of Manatí, the first to take this line, was rejected. Embarrassed by the new resistance techniques, the army rejected many young men on a variety of grounds. As the resistance grew, and FUPI endorsed the rejection of such loyalty oaths in 1964, the Selective Service system ordered that *independentistas* be inducted.

This was the setting of the Alvelo Case. Sixto Alvelo, a young Aibonito worker, pioneered by flatly refusing to join the North Americans' army, and others followed his example. Alvelo's stance and MPI's support started a general tide of protest against military service. The campaign undertaken by *independentista* organizations, and by the committee formed to support young men who faced U. S. federal court trials, achieved its aim.* The federal prosecutor in San Juan withdrew the charges against Alvelo and seven others on a legal technicality.

Out of the Alvelo Case came one of the most popular, mass-supported campaigns in Puerto Rican history. The young people's rejection of military service took many active forms: picketing Selective Service offices, lampoons, national and local demonstrations, etc. The protest grew from defiance to open illegal struggle. There were declarations of political and legal support for any youth refusing to serve, mass repudiations of the law in towns, schools, and at the University, open declarations of solidarity with Vietnam's National Liberation Front. The hundreds of young men hounded, arrested, and suspended from school or fired from jobs all dramatized the breadth of the resistance and of our people's awareness of what they were resisting—and both continued to broaden. In 1968 the Selective Service reported 1,000 "delinquents" in Puerto

---

* As this is written, the Alvelo Committee for Defense of Puerto Rican Youth has been organized in ten districts and municipalities. Its chairman is Dr. Piri Fernández de Lewis and its board includes such distinguished intellectuals as Dr. Isabel Gutiérrez del Arroyo, Dr. Margot Arce de Vázquez, Dr. José Ferrer Canales, Dr. Manuel Maldonado Denis, Licenciado Nilita Vientos Gastón, José Antonio Torres Martinó, and René Marqués.

Rico alone who had not responded to orders to report for military duty.*

This experience helped to awaken national and class consciousness. The ruling classes controlling the Selective Service boards used all their power to keep their children and families out of the army, altering the lists so that these would instead enter the Reserves or the National Guard. For the poor it was a demonstration of who would be used as cannon-fodder. And the high proportion of youth in our population ensures that the fight against military service will continue to be one of the key battles in our liberation struggle.†.

Under the symbolic sign of fire the Armed Commandos of Liberation (CAL) emerged in 1967. This was a qualitative step forward in the struggle, marking the first appearance of clandestine armed resistance in Puerto Rico.‡ CAL's targets were foreign investments and U. S. monopolies: they aimed at undermining the imperialist power-base in the island, to hasten a crisis which would shake the foundations of the Puerto Rican colonial world and enable the struggle to move on to the offensive and toward

---

* As a result of the demonstrations and picket lines many members of Selective Service boards in the towns have recently resigned. In some towns the boards are not functioning because the members have resigned and replacements cannot be found.

† At the time of writing more than 300 military-age youths are awaiting federal court trials for resisting military service.

‡ The appearance of a clandestine force which the government has not been able to control has led to greater polarization of the struggle. The police have launched a repressive campaign against *independentista* groups, violating civil rights and fabricating evidence, which shows the hysteria in official circles. Participating in this campaign are the FBI, local intelligence services, military intelligence, and the CIA, which has offices over the Chase Manhattan Bank in Río Piedras. The FBI's offices are in the Pan American building in Hato Rey.

victory. With Woolworth's, Pueblo Supermarkets, Kresge, Sears Roebuck, Bargain Town, Grand Union, K-Mart, and other U. S. enterprises as military objectives, CAL responded to the special economic and geographic characteristics of our society. It proclaimed the Condado as its "war zone," * and created a climate of insecurity which ended colonial peace and imperiled foreign investment. With regard to military service CAL announced: "We will not lose sight of the real enemy, the Yanqui imperialists, for we have a commitment which we renew today before the patriotic people of Puerto Rico: FOR EVERY YOUNG PUERTO RICAN JAILED FOR REFUSING TO SERVE IN THE U. S. ARMED FORCES, WE WILL EXECUTE A YANQUI." [75] CAL thus declared its intention to pursue a policy of personal terrorism against the enemy. After the above announcement, no North American could feel secure in Puerto Rico.†

The proliferation of CAL actions threatens the whole colonial power structure. It is the start of the armed confrontation which the colonialists fear so much, coming at a time when the first holes are beginning to show in the stability of the colonial regime.

In the 1968 elections the liberal-autonomist Popular

---

* The Condado is one of the country's chief tourist areas. There are no precise figures for the losses caused by CAL sabotage but they are known to be in the neighborhood of $100 million.

† The question of violence and terrorism produced a crisis among the Marxists in MPI which led to the ousting from the party of César Andreu Iglesias, Samuel Aponte, and George From. This group publishes the theoretical political journal *La Escalera*. CAL now advocates an escalated policy of ten attacks for every one act of repression by the government. The government has not been able to stop CAL's activities. Bombs continue to explode in Condado hotels, fires break out in various U. S. offices and installations. The most recent bombing incidents were in the Hotel San Juan and Isla Verde's Hotel Americana in February 1971. A parallel clandestine group in New York, the Movimiento Independentista Revolucionario Armado (MIRA), has also been active.

Party experienced its biggest crisis: after controlling national politics for twenty-eight years, it lost by more than 30,000 votes to the capitalist Ferré's New Progressive Party. This produced a new political situation in the country—an imbalance of power, a new scramble for position, and an unfreezing of the colonial bureaucratic structure. Autonomism as a transitory regime headed for its natural denouement.*

The greater the effectiveness of CAL, the more repression has been stepped up in the colony. CAL's actions, the instability the system began to display, the activities of *independentista* organizations with their campaigns of defiance, the campaign against military service and the ROTC, and the general resistance which this promoted— all these widened the contradiction between system and people. The ideological line and the united actions on organizational and mass levels guided the development of MPI from a patriotic vanguard toward a revolutionary vanguard. Beyond this, CAL promotes a psychological liberation. It gives content to a struggle which has continued for 100 years. It gives the lie to the colonial thesis about our "incapacity." It unmasks those who have thrived under the shade of the colonial tree.

The crisis of the colonial structure which we aim to produce will bring independence in its wake. We will

---

* The service performed by liberal autonomism was purely transitory. When it had achieved its aim of crushing Nationalism it lost its *raison d'être* and had to be replaced by a more reactionary, unconditional, and anti-national administration. See *Claridad*, November 23, 1969, p. 6.

The New Progressive Party "won" the government and control of the House by a narrow margin of two representatives, while the Popular Party controlled the Senate. One-third of the municipalities are controlled by the former, the rest by the latter. The New Progressive Party won in mainly urban, the Popular Party in mainly rural, areas.

achieve it by intensifying legal, openly illegal, and clandestine activities. Dissolution of the colony will come through *struggle*. To this people fighting today under the banner of "Independence or Death!" preparing, as Che said, "to intone our funeral dirge with the staccato of machine-guns and new cries of battle and victory," we say:

EVER ONWARD TO VICTORY!

Notes

1. Malcolm X, "On Afro-American History," *International Socialist Review,* March–April 1967, p. 4.
2. Jean-Paul Sartre, "Introduction" to Frantz Fanon, *The Wretched of the Earth* (New York: Grove Press, 1962), p. 13.
3. See Alejandro Tapia y Rivera, *La Palma del Cacique* (San Juan, 1943), and Manuel Méndez Ballester, *Isla Cerrera* (San Juan, 1938).
4. Salvador Brau, *Historia: La colonización de Puerto Rico* (San Juan: Instituto de Cultura Puertorriqueña, 1966), p. 142.
5. Friedrich Engels, *Anti-Dühring* (New York: International Publishers, 1939), p. 202.
6. Miguel Meléndez Muñoz, *El Jíbaro en el Siglo XIX* (San Juan: Ediciones Rumbos, 1963), p. 32.
7. Ibid., p. 143.
8. Ibid.
9. Lidio Cruz Monclova, *Historia de Puerto Rico (Siglo XIX),* Vol. III (Río Piedras: Ediciones de la Universidad de Puerto Rico, 1958), p. 376.
10. For further clarification of this, see Lidio Cruz Monclova, ibid., and his two other works, *Baldorioty de Castro* and *Luis Muñoz Rivera: Diez años de su vida,* both published by the Instituto de Cultura Puertorriqueña.
11. Mariano Abril and Tomás Carrión Maduro quoted by Lidio Cruz Monclova, op. cit., pp. 357 and 373.
12. Francisco Manrique Cabrera, *Historia de la Literatura Puertorriqueña* (New York: Las Americas Publishing Co., 1956), p. 134.
13. Aníbal Ponce, *De Erasmo a Romain Rolland* (Buenos Aires: Editorial Futuro, 1962), p. 121.
14. Ibid., p. 85.
15. Luis Muñoz Rivera, *Obras Completas: January–December 1893* (San Juan: Instituto de Cultura Puertorriqueña, 1966), pp. 9–10.
16. Margot Arce de Vázquez, *Impresiones* (San Juan: Editorial Yaurel, 1950), pp. 29, 120.

17. Georges Politzer, *Cursos de Filosofía* (Mexico: Fondo de Cultura Popular, 1962), p. 182.
18. Richard Levins, "La Batalla de las Ideas," *La Escalera*, March 1967, p. 11.
19. See René Marqués, "The Sound and Fury of the Critics of Mr. Kazin," *Ensayos, 1953–1966* (San Juan: Ediciones Antillana, 1967), p. 119.
20. César Andreu Iglesias, *Independencia y Socialismo* (San Juan: Librería Estrella Roja, 1951), p. 38.
21. Tomás Blanco, *Prontuario Histórico* (San Juan: Biblioteca de Autores Puertorriqueños, 1946), p. 113.
22. Gordon Lewis, *Puerto Rico: Freedom and Power in the Caribbean* (New York: Monthly Review Press, 1963), p. 116.
23. César Andreu Iglesias, op. cit., p. 38.
24. Thomas C. Cochran, *El hombre de Negocios Puertorriqueño* (University of Puerto Rico: Centro de Investigaciones Sociales, 1961), p. 28.
25. Ibid., p. 21.
26. Karl Marx and Friedrich Engels, *The Communist Manifesto* (New York: Monthly Review Press, 1968), p. 7.
27. Aníbal Ponce, op. cit., p. 35.
28. Manuel Fraga Iribarne, *Las Constituciones de Puerto Rico* (Madrid: Ediciones Cultura Hispánica, 1953), p. 41.
29. Quoted by Reece B. Bothwell, *Trasfondo Constitucional de Puerto Rico* (Río Piedras: Ediciones de la Universidad de Puerto Rico, 1966), p. 45.
30. Theodore Roosevelt, *Fifth Annual Message*, December 5, 1905.
31. José de Diego, *Obras Completas*, Vol. III (San Juan: Instituto de Cultura Puertorriqueña, 1966), p. 233.
32. Ibid., p. 241.
33. *Congressional Record*, House, Vol. 53, May 5, 1916, p. 7471.
34. José de Diego, op. cit., pp. 345–346.
35. Ibid., p. 282.
36. Ibid., pp. 529–530.
37. Juan Antonio Corretjer, *Hostos y Albizu Campos* (Guaynabo, 1965).
38. Bolívar Pagán, *Historia de los Partidos Políticos Puertorriqueños*, Vol. II (San Juan: Librería Campos, 1959), p. 53.
39. See Curzio Malaparte, *Técnica del Golpe de Estado* (Madrid: Ediciones Ulises, 1931).

40. Robert Taber, *La Guerra de la Pulga* (Mexico: Ediciones ERA, 1967), p. 102.
41. César Andreu Iglesias, *La Escalera,* January–February 1968, p. 11.
42. Ibid., p. 18.
43. William Z. Foster, *History of the Communist Party of the United States* (New York: International Publishers, 1952), p. 337.
44. René Marqués, "El Puertorriqueño Dócil," *Cuadernos Americanos* (Mexico), January–February 1962, p. 159. See also Isabel Gutiérrez del Arroyo, *Puerto Rico, Estado federado? Razones de una sinrazón* (San Juan, 1960).
45. Frantz Fanon, op. cit., p. 47.
46. *La Democracia,* January 27, 1940, p. 12.
47. Eduardo Seda Bonilla, *Interacción Social y Personalidad en una Comunidad en Puerto Rico* (San Juan: Ediciones Juan Ponce de León, 1964), p. 117.
48. Luis Nieves Falcón, "El Futuro Ideólogico del Partido Popular Democrático," *Revista de Ciencias Sociales,* September 3, 1965.
49. Ibid., p. 261.
50. For details, see Ramón Ramírez, *La Historia del Movimiento Libertador en la Historia de Puerto Rico,* Vol. II (San Juan: Imprenta Borinquen, 1954); and Manuel Maldonado Denis, *Puerto Rico: Una Interpretacion Historico-Social* (Mexico: Editiones Siglo XXI, 1969).
51. Richard Levins, "De Rebelde a Revolucionario," *La Escalera,* April–May 1966, p. 16.
52. Manuel Maldonado Denis, "Declinar del Movimiento Independentista Puertorriqueño?" *Revista de Ciencias Sociales,* September 1965, p. 294.
53. René Marqués, op. cit.
54. Ho Chi Minh, "The Counter-Revolutionary Army," *Selected Works* (Havana: Tricontinental, 1968), p. 68.
55. José A. Herrero, "The Effects of Minimum Wage Legislation on the Rate of Growth and Employment of the Puerto Rican Economy," p. 4. (Mimeographed.)
56. Harvey S. Perloff, *Puerto Rico's Economic Picture* (Chicago: University of Chicago Press, 1949).
57. José Herrero, op. cit.
58. Rolando Castañeda and José A. Herrero, "La Distribución del

134 *We, the Puerto Rican People*

Ingreso en Puerto Rico: Un Estudio Realizado en Base a los Años 1953–1963 ," pp. 13–14. (Mimeographed.)

59. Eduardo Seda Bonilla, "La Jueyera: Enajenación y Seudoconflicto," p. 6. (Mimeographed.)

60. See the thesis of acquired docility in René Marqués, "The Sound and Fury of the Critics of Mr. Kazin," op. cit., p. 119.

61. Juan José Osuna, *A History of Education in Puerto Rico* (Río Piedras: Ediciones de la Universidad de Puerto Rico, 1949), p. 281.

62. See Luis Muñiz Soufront. *El Problema del Idoma en Puerto Rico* (San Juan: Biblioteca de Autores Puertorriqueños, 1950).

63. The effort was published under the title *La Escuela Pública en Puerto Rico: Normas de Supervisión y Administración Escolar* (Department of Education, 1954).

64. See *Preámbulo de la Constitución del Estado Libre Asociado.*

65. Aníbal Ponce, *Educación y Lucha de Clases* (Havana: Imprenta Nacional de Cuba, 1961), p. 35.

66. Ibid.

67. See Luis Nieves Falcón, *Recruitment to Higher Education in Puerto Rico, 1940–1960* (Río Piedras: Ediciones de la Universidad de Puerto Rico, 1965).

68. Karl Marx, *Capital,* Vol. I (London: Lawrence & Wishart, 1970), pp. 354–355.

69. Richard Levins, "La Batalla de las Ideas," *La Escalera,* March 1967, p. 11.

70. Richard Levins, "De Rebelde a Revolucionario," op. cit., p. 5.

71. Ibid.

72. *Tesis Política MPI, Supplement* (1964), "Despierta, Boricua; defiende lo tuyo!"

73. Frantz Fanon, op. cit., p. 30.

74. Juan Mari Bras, in a letter to the author, February 24, 1967.

75. *Tricontinental, Supplement* (1968), p. 6.

Selected Monthly Review Paperbacks

The Age of Imperialism by Harry Magdoff $ 5.50

Capitalist Patriarchy and the Case For Socialist Feminism,
edited by Zillah R. Eisenstein 7.50

China Since Mao by Charles Bettelheim and Neil Burton 3.95

Columbus: His Enterprise by Hans Koning 4.95

Death on the Job by Daniel Berman 7.50

The Disinherited: Journal of a Palestinian Exile by Fawaz Turki 5.95

Dynamics of Global Crisis by Samir Amin, Giovanni Arrighi,
Andre Gunder Frank, and Immanuel Wallerstein 7.50

The End of Prosperity by Harry Magdoff and Paul M. Sweezy 2.95

The Growth of the Modern West Indies by Gordon K. Lewis 9.50

Imperialism: From the Colonial Age to the Present
by Harry Magdoff 5.00

Introduction to the Sociology of "Developing Societies,"
edited by Hamza Alavi and Teodor Shanin 12.50

Karl Marx's Theory of Revolution. Vol. 1: State and Bureaucracy
(2 vols. in one) by Hal Draper 9.50

Karl Marx's Theory of Revolution. Vol. 2: The Politics
of Social Classes by Hal Draper 12.95

Labor and Monopoly Capital by Harry Braverman 7.00

Latin America: Underdevelopment or Revolution
by Andre Gunder Frank 6.50

Let Me Speak! Testimony of Domitila, A Woman of the Bolivian
Mines by Domitila Barrios de Chungara with Moema Viezzer 6.50

The Long Default by William K. Tabb 6.95

The Long Transition by Idrian Resnick 10.00

Man's Worldly Goods by Leo Huberman 8.00

Marxist Economic Theory by Ernest Mandel (2 vols.) 13.00

Monopoly Capital by Paul A. Baran and Paul M. Sweezy 6.50

Myth of Population Control: Family, Caste, and Class
in an Indian Village by Mahmood Mamdani 4.50

On the Transition to Socialism
by Paul M. Sweezy and Charles Bettelheim 6.00

The People's Republic of China: A Documentary History of
Revolutionary Change, edited by Mark Selden 15.00

The Political Economy of Growth by Paul A. Baran 7.50

The Poverty of Theory and Other Essays by E.P. Thompson 6.50

Protest and Survive, edited by E.P. Thompson and Dan Smith 4.95

The Ragged Trousered Philanthropists by Robert Tressell 7.50

The Road to Gdansk by Daniel Singer 6.50

The Scalpel, the Sword: The Story of Dr. Norman Bethune
by Sidney Gordon and Ted Allan 5.95

The Struggle for Zimbabwe by David Martin and Phyllis Johnson 8.95

The Theory of Capitalist Development by Paul M. Sweezy 7.50

The Third World in World Economy by Pierre Jalée 4.50

Toward an Anthropology of Women, edited by Rayna R. Reiter 7.50

Unequal Development by Samir Amin 8.50

Unity and Struggle: Speeches and Writings by Amilcar Cabral 10.00

Wasi'chu: The Continuing Indian Wars
by Bruce Johansen and Roberto Maestas 6.95